TWELVE MIME PLAYS

THE BRIDESMAIDS
IN 'THE MARRIAGE OF COLUMBINE'
From 'Modes de Paris,' 1838

TWELVE MIME PLAYS

A COLLECTION OF WORDLESS
PLAYS ARRANGED TO MUSIC

BY

IRENE MAWER

WITH EIGHT PLATES AND
EIGHT ILLUSTRATIONS IN THE TEXT

METHUEN & CO. LTD.
36 ESSEX STREET W.C.
LONDON

First Published in 1933

PRINTED IN GREAT BRITAIN

INTRODUCTION

These plays are intended, primarily, for the use of teachers, and for producers working with students or amateur players. Most of them have already been performed and have been proved practicable for varied casts and audiences. Each will be found to have a marked pictorial value, necessitating the study of period and costume, while the simplest settings will form the required background. Many can be played successfully in the open air.

It should, however, be realized that the Mime Play is a complete art form and cannot be attempted without a technical knowledge of the art of Mime on the part of both the producer and players. A Mime is not merely a pageant or a spoken play with the words left out ; it is the finished example of a highly technical branch of Drama.

These plays, it is hoped, may be found useful to the teacher or producer who wishes to bring to the pitch of performance the work which has already been studied in detail.

The play form is particularly valuable in emphasizing the essential dramatic significance of the art of Mime. It unites students or children in a common endeavour, and engenders sympathy, generosity, unself-consciousness and a sense of 'giving', while individual idiosyncrasies are sunk in the production as a whole.

The producer or teacher should insist that every member of the cast shall fully appreciate the period in which the play is set. Before beginning to rehearse, the characteristic movements of the different parts in the given period should be studied. Costume and properties should not be added, somewhat haphazard, at a dress rehearsal. Every character should be able to describe the essential points of his or her costume from the first rehearsal. Properties should, in the same way, be given their due importance, historical correctness and dramatic significance. All this proves a valuable factor in historical study, where the play is to be performed as part of a school or college curriculum, and, in the case of professional players, gives that sureness of touch without which a Mime Play must inevitably fail of its effect.

The question of the music must also receive due consideration and study. The music has, as far as possible, been chosen for its appropriateness in period, type, colour, and dramatic force, while retaining, at the same time, a necessary simplicity of form, suitable to the inexperienced Mime actor. For the music is no extraneous accompaniment. No player can be said to have studied his or her part until capable of rendering in movement or expression every bar of every musical phrase.

The producer is urged to study, not only the outline of the ' story ', the development of plot and character within the given convention, but also the musical numbers in their sequence, before attempting to rehearse any part of the play.

The teacher will find helpful the chapter on The Construction and Teaching of Mime Plays in my companion volume, *The Art of Mime*, while the technical and historical sections of that book deal with those aspects as shown in the plays.

The Mime Play is a difficult dramatic form. There is, sometimes, a tendency among inexperienced producers to say, ' Let us do a Mime ; it is so much easier than a spoken play ; and you don't have to learn any words.' But where one may see a dozen adequate performances of a spoken play one will not find one good Mime. This is generally due to the fact that people will happily embark upon the production of a Mime when not one member of the cast can make the simplest remark in really clear gesture, while the most elementary aspects of silent acting have not been studied. In this way nothing is made clear to the audience, who gain a vague impression that the scene is ' pretty ' or ' amusing ', but are left to guess what it is all about.

The producer should remember that the connexion between audience and players is *visual*, that every detail must be as clearly and concisely *stated* in gesture and movement as it would be in words in the spoken play. Above all, the interest must be centralized. No one, however well intentioned, can be looking at two things at once. Consequently, only one thing must happen at a time, and even the slightest movement on the part of a minor character must have some bearing upon the significance, at a given moment, of the central figures. Let the Mime actor learn first to stand still, to be significant in repose, never to make an unnecessary movement ; and, finally, when he does move, to do so rhythmically, decisively, and unmistakably.

The value of grouping must be realized, in order that every climax in the play may be focused pictorially upon the vision of the audience. A Mime Play must be a synchronizing of music and action, otherwise the audience registers one thing by sound and another by sight.

It is my hope that, if these plays are studied sincerely and painstakingly, they may prove a source of pleasure to producer and performer alike. Many of them have been written to satisfy the needs of a given group of students or as an item in a particular programme. At least they have been made and rehearsed by one whose work and study during some fifteen years have been to meet the needs of students, children, and audiences of many types and varied enthusiasms. If the plays find new friends, now that they are gathered together in this form, I shall feel that the task of assembling them has been as happy a one as was the creating of each in its turn.

IRENE MAWER

CONTENTS

ix

PLAYS FOR CHILDREN

LIST OF PLATES

LIST OF
ILLUSTRATIONS IN THE TEXT

* *Reproduced by courtesy of the Proprietors of 'Punch'*
† *Reproduced from 'Manners, Customs, and Dress during the Middle Ages' by Paul Lacroix (Bickers & Son).*

GENERAL NOTES ON
THE ARRANGEMENT OF THE MUSIC

The marginal letters in the text refer to the musical numbers as given at the end of each play.

The various musical selections should be procured and arranged in the correct order, with cuts clearly marked.

The movements should then be worked out in barring as given in the notes. It is as well to write on the musical score the exact movements for each phrase. The producer will then have two prompt copies—one giving the details of plot and stage movements ; the other the bare outline of essential moves, together with the music.

Conversely, the pianist should be in possession of the printed text, in order to appreciate the dramatic significance of each musical number.

As far as possible each member of the cast should also have a copy of the text of the play, in order to be able to study and learn the exact order of movements, and the musical barring connected with them.

NOTES ON COSTUME

Costume lists and property plots will be found at the end of each play.

These are given rather as an indication of style and period than as hard and fast rules. Each producer or costume designer will vary details and colour effects to suit his own tastes.

ACKNOWLEDGMENTS AND ADDRESSES

I wish to express my thanks to the following Music Publishers for permission to quote the various musical selections. Their addresses are given in order to avoid any delay in ordering the required numbers :

Messrs. Boosey & Hawkes, 295 Regent Street, London, W. 1. Selling Agents for Hawkes & Son, Ltd., and Winthrop Rogers, Ltd.

Messrs. J. Curwen & Sons, Ltd., 24 Berners Street, London, W. 1.

Messrs. Alfred Lengnick & Co., Ltd., 14 Berners Street, London, W. 1.

Messrs. J. & W. Chester, Ltd., 11 Great Marlborough Street, London, W. 1.

Messrs. Elkin & Co., Ltd., 20 Kingly Street, Regent Street, London, W. 1.

Messrs. Augener & Co., Ltd., 18 Great Marlborough Street, London, W. 1.

Messrs. Walsh, 51 High Street, London, W.C. 2.

Messrs. Ascherberg, Hopwood & Crew, 16 Mortimer Street, London, W. 1.

Messrs. J. B. Cramer & Co., Ltd., 139 New Bond Street, London, W. 1.

In the case of a public performance of any of the plays, permission for the use of the music should be obtained from :

THE PERFORMING RIGHT SOCIETY, 13 George Street, Hanover Square, London, W. 1.

Permission for performance of the plays must be obtained from :

THE SECRETARY, THE GINNER-MAWER SCHOOL OF DANCE AND DRAMA, Philbeach Hall, Philbeach Gardens, S.W.5.

THE PIERROTS AT VERSAILLES

(Music selected from the works of Schumann and F. Swinstead.)

The play has been performed at the Arts Theatre, the Rudolf Steiner Hall, at pastoral performances at Stratford-on-Avon and Malvern, and in the Ginner-Mawer Performances in Hyde Park under the auspices of the League of Arts, 1930, 1931.

The original cast was as follows :

Pierrot Blanc	.. .. ..	*Irene Mawer*
Pierrot Noir	.. ..	*Joyce Ruscoe*
Madame la Marquise	.. ..	*Lesley Hodson*
Monsieur le Marquis..	.. ..	*Evelyn Doak*
The Negro Servant ..	.. ..	*Margaret Rubel*
Jeunes Filles	.. ..	{ *Mary Wardrop* { *Kathleen Scott*

The play was in all instances produced by the author.

THE PIERROTS AT VERSAILLES

The moon shines upon the Gardens of Versailles. The shadows are full of mystery, the glades are wonder-lit, for we are in the eighteenth century, when every lady was a poem, perfect in form, from her high-heeled shoes to the rosebud hidden under the top-most curl of her elaborate coiffure. The gardens and the ladies are such as Watteau knew, and he has shown us that where there are lovely ladies among the trees, there is almost sure to be the wondering, wide-eyed figure of a Pierrot, bringing into the conventional atmosphere of the Court the childlike simplicity of the peasant. Here, then, are ladies, one especially exquisite, and two Pierrots, each white-faced, but one dressed in black, the other in white. Where there is a lady we may be sure there is a lord, so the characters are :

> Pierrot Blanc
> Pierrot Noir
> Madame la Marquise
> Monsieur le Marquis
> Jeunes Filles
> A Negro Servant

The Scene is a glade in the Gardens with a terrace at the back, beyond which burns the night sky. Against the sky are silhouetted two formal trees. Down right is a stone seat. The light of the full moon makes everything as clear as day, yet more romantic.

A.   From among the shadows, up left, flit two moth-like figures ; they are the Jeunes Filles, little ladies-in-waiting upon Madame la Marquise. They float into the moonlight, rest for a moment down left, their heads, crowned with rose-wreaths, laid close together, for the exchange of some piece of delicious scandal. Then they are away again, up to the back, where two fingers laid on two pairs of lips hush back the little gurgles of mischief we half expect to hear, as out from the

3

darkness drifts the exquisite figure of la Marquise herself. She has wandered into the gardens, half in love with the beauty of the night, to enjoy the romantic experience of reading a book of poems by moonlight. As she passes on, the little girls slip away out of sight, and she is left alone in the glade and the moonlight.

What a picture! The beautiful lady, the moonlight, the shadowed trees; and how well she knows that she perfectly befits this perfect moment.

She drifts like some stately galleon down left, crosses to the seat, glances at the book, wanders up to the terrace, and, at last, floats away once more, to other moonlit spaces, leaving our picture empty of all save the memory of her, that is like the sound of some old minuet played gravely, but with a haunting sweetness.

B.   Only for a moment is the picture empty, for hardly has la Marquise disappeared, than a white figure steals on from up right. It is Pierrot Blanc, afraid of the shadows, afraid of the moon, afraid of the stately, courtly place, but drawn by the vision of the sweet face of the Marquise as he saw it when he watched her unseen. In his arms is a sheaf of white lilies. Somehow he must find her and lay them at her feet, and declare to her the passion that stirs under his white coat. He tiptoes with long, cautious steps across the back; then turns in a panic, to find his own shadow following him. He retreats to the safety of the trees whence he came. Once more he cautiously reaches the centre of the terrace, where he stands gazing in the direction in which the Marquise disappeared. His back is to the audience, so he fails to see, as we do, another white face appear. This time it is down left, and cautiously, cautiously Pierrot Noir crawls out from the bushes, also in terror of the night, yet drawn on by the irresistible vision of the Marquise. He carries with infinite care the poem which he will lay at her feet when at last he meets her and can tell her of the love that burns under his black coat. He crawls to the centre front, then darts back again into the shadows. Again he creeps forward, this time right across the front to the opposite proscenium, where he remains peering into the shadows, for unknown dangers, or wondering which way his vision really disappeared.

Now Pierrot Blanc begins to move again. This time he tiptoes to up left and peers between the trees. Each Pierrot thinks he sees some one coming, and, with desperate care, retreats backwards towards the centre. They hold their breaths ; every step is anxiously taken. Till, horror ! each meets some unknown person with a sickening bump. Ghosts ! Gendarmes ! Fire ! Murder !

Without stopping to see with what they have collided, they dart away into the shadows by the proscenium, Pierrot Blanc down left, Pierrot Noir down right. They hide their terrified eyes against the tree-trunks (which are the proscenium as we see it). Slowly, as nothing further happens, they each peer out. There is a suspicious form over there. Ghost ? Gendarme ? No ! Frère Pierrot ! A thousand thunders ! The intruder, the base spoil-sport ! Courage returns with rage. Each says simultaneously (they have a maddening habit of saying the same thing at the same moment), ' You ! '

Enraged and dignified they advance towards each other. They stand together, centre, the picture of two naughty children playing at being outraged heroes of romance.

C.   Pierrot Noir, with dignity, inquires, ' You here ? Why ? ' Pierrot Blanc coldly answers, ' *You* here ? Why ? ' Pierrot Noir says emphatically, ' You go away.' Pierrot Blanc replies, ' On the contrary, I shall stay just here.' Then they speak together, ' You and I, why are we here, anyway ? ' And with a knowing look they answer themselves, ' The exquisite lady walks here, that's why.' Then Pierrot Noir, as one settling the question for ever, says, ' I have written this perfect poem for her.' But Pierrot Blanc merely replies with a greater flourish, ' And I have brought her these most exquisite lilies.' Together they sigh in ecstatic fervour, ' I *adore* her ! '

Their gesture is superb. Their fears are gone. The moonlight shines on two small forms transfigured and tense with emotion.

D.   But hark ! Some one is coming. Their heroics collapse.

Once more two terrified figures dash for the proscenium trees,
as a delicate little air steals into our ears, and into our sight
there floats again the figure of one of the girls. She is followed
almost immediately by the Negro *laquais*, then by the Marquise herself, followed by the second girl. The Marquise
reclines on the seat and bids the girls settle on the grass beside
her. And there they are, just like some Watteau picture,
alight with laughter and faint scandalous deliciousness.

The Pierrots creep from their hiding-places, up to the back,
whence each hopes to have a better view of his adored. So
engrossed with his own cautious progress is each that they
find themselves tiptoeing straight into the grotesque and
alarming form of the Negro servant, who, though small, is a
terrifying object to a love-lorn Pierrot. His eyes roll white
in his black face ; the intruders disappear hastily behind the
trees right and left of the centre back.

Now the Marquise speaks graciously to the girls. ' Play
your games of cat's-cradle, my children.' She smiles, and
motions the servant to come forward. Obediently, he comes,
with fantastic tread, bearing upon a silver tray a length of
scarlet ribbon. He bows, presents the ribbon to the first
girl, and retires once more to his place. The girls play at
cat's-cradle together, while the Marquise watches them
graciously. She does not notice that two white faces are
watching her, first from behind the trees, and then from
behind the Negro servant as he stands immovable, save for
the rolling and suspicious eyes.

At last one of the girls tangles the ribbon, and, tired of the
game, throws it down and runs, petulantly, out of sight.
The other asks the Marquise's permission to follow her. The
lady motions her away, and bids the servant begone, too, so
that she may be left alone a little with her book.

The Pierrots, in an agony of hope, watch his pompous
exit, and each prepares to be left alone with the object of his
passion. As usual, they have forgotten each other !

E.   The Marquise sits dreamily upon the seat. Pierrot Noir,
with splendid step and gesture, places himself in the best
position to call attention to himself and to approach her

'PIERROT CONTENT,' BY WATTEAU

COSTUMES FOR PIERROT BLANC AND MARQUISE IN 'THE PIERROTS AT VERSAILLES'

with suitable dignity. He stands a second up left, prepared to make the first step, when—Pierrot Blanc dashes in front of him with the same intent, and they advance simultaneously, Pierrot Blanc leading. But Pierrot Noir will not bear it. He catches Pierrot Blanc by the shoulder and draws him back to the starting-point, placing himself ostentatiously in front. Once more they advance slowly and simultaneously. By now the Marquise has seen them, and is much intrigued by the curious little manikins that have appeared in her garden so suddenly.

Before Pierrot Noir can speak, his rival has dragged him back once more, and stands centre, saying, ' Madame, *I* have brought these lilies for your acceptance ' ; and he kneels to give his offering. But Pierrot Noir has dashed round to the other side of the seat where *he* is, saying, ' But *I* have brought you this exquisite poem.'

At the same moment they rise, and each taking what he believes to be the centre of the stage, announces, ' I love you.' The last flourish of their splendid gesture brings them face to face. They have spoken, not to the Marquise, but to each other ! Their rage finds vent in a resounding if some-what childish stamp, which brings them heroically back to back. Tableaux.

The Marquise rises. These charming children must not spoil the beauty of the night by quarrelling in her garden. Besides, they are amusing. She will look at them closer. So she comes round behind them and taps them simultaneously on the shoulders.

They spring apart, each saying to himself, ' Ah, she has noticed me.' She sweeps between them, shaking a cautionary finger, and circles the stage, they following eagerly.

Once more she lingers centre. Each Pierrot says to himself, ' This is my chance.' They prepare ; they speak. ' I love you,' they say, as they fling themselves upon one knee, offering their gifts to the Marquise, who finds them both adorably entertaining. She bends to each and graciously accepts their offerings.

But, heavens, some one is coming ! The Marquise is a little flustered ; the Pierrots are alarmed. She flies to the

seat; they stand a moment behind it; and, then, to be sure
that no unfair advantages are taken, each extinguishes the
other by placing a hand on his head and pushing his rival
out of sight behind the back of the seat.

F.   Only just in time. The Negro servant returns, establishes
himself centre back with his accustomed fantastic dignity,
and announces, ' Monsieur is on his way here.'

The Marquise is amused at the situation in which she finds
herself. But the heads of two alarmed Pierrots rise from
behind her. ' Hush ! ' she says to them in turn ; and once
more they extinguish each other.

The Marquise, with a twinkle of enjoyment in her adorable
eyes, takes two red roses from the breast of her gown ; one
she slips into the centre of White Pierrot's sheaf of lilies, the
other she folds into the scroll of Black Pierrot's poem. Then
she sits, exquisitely composed, to await the arrival of Monsieur
le Marquis.

He appears, gloriously apparelled, and followed by the
two Jeunes Filles, in a twitter of excitement. ' M. le Marquis
is so handsome and he is sure to have brought some beautiful
offering for Madame la Marquise.' He has. He opens the
leather case he carries, lifts from it a priceless necklace of
diamonds, and handing the case nonchalantly to the servant,
offers the necklace to Madame with a bow of the purest
gallantry. With what a grace she accepts it and lays it round
her snowy neck for him to admire. But he has yet another
gift for her. From his own finger he draws a ring of beautiful
workmanship. It sparkles richly as he places it on her hand.
Madame is delighted. Such taste, such perfect manners.
Now, M. le Marquis offers her the tips of his exquisite fingers
and asks her to accept his company within doors. Together,
like two expensive puppets moved by invisible strings, they
pass away out of sight. The little girls are left to sigh, ' Ah !
what a husband ! ' and to follow at a discreet distance. The
servant follows also, with the leisured indolence of one whose
work is accomplished, and who is about to join the gentlemen's
gentlemen.

The Pierrots are alone once more. Two white, dejected

faces have watched the little scene of the return of the most unsatisfactory wealthy husband of the object of their adoration. As the Marquise passes out of sight, they are left, still kneeling behind the seat, only their heads showing above it, each saying the fatal word, ' Married ! ' Tableaux of despair.

G.   Pierrot Blanc rises dejectedly. He walks slowly and sadly to the centre and up towards the back. Then he turns. He remembers the sheaf of white lilies. He might as well take them with him. She forgot them—hardly noticed them in fact—but they were good lilies and it is a pity to waste them. He returns, slowly picks up the bouquet, and as slowly returns to centre. There his grief overcomes him. He sniffs, his shoulders heave, he sobs in time to the music.

Now Pierrot Noir rises. He catches sight of the poem he wrote for Her. He cannot leave it behind to be scorned, perhaps, or merely overlooked. He picks it up. Then his grief breaks out, and he, too, sobs, by the corner of the seat, in time to the music.

Adversity is a great softener of the temper. The two Pierrots catch sight of each other. Still weeping bitterly, Pierrot Blanc holds out his arms ; Pierrot Noir staggers into them. They sob with great energy in each other's arms, still in time to the music.

H.   When—suddenly—light breaks. Each sees, over the other's shoulder, his own offering, and nestling in the centre of it a deep red rose. Breathless with excitement, and once more oblivious of each other, they draw out the precious emblems. Exultant, they circle the stage until they arrive once more back to back, where they speak again together in the splendid gesture of well-earned triumph, ' She loves *me* ! '

Success can afford to be magnanimous. Rivalry is forgotten. Generous, each in the joy of his own supposed success, they remember one another, and holding the precious roses in their free hands, they embrace fervently. ' Brother,' they say, ' Brother ! '

And the moon laughs on the Pierrots in the Gardens at Versailles.

NOTES ON MUSIC

Music Required :

Nachtstücke. Opus 23	..	..	..	Schumann
Fantasiestücke. Opus 111	..	..	..	Schumann
My Ladye's Minuet	..	..	..	F. Swinstead

(All published by Augener & Co., Ltd.)

A.   *Nachtstücke.* No. 3.   *The Vision of the Marquise*

Repeat first 8 bars. Play to 32nd bar. Cut to end

Curtain music	8 bars
Entrance of Girls	8 bars
Entrance of Marquise—her moves and exit ..	24 bars

B.   *Nachtstücke.* No. 1.   *Entrance of the Pierrots*

Play 32 bars. Cut to end

Entrance of Pierrot Blanc	8 bars
Entrance of Pierrot Noir	8 bars
Both to up left and down right and meet centre ..	8 bars
Run away to corners, see each other, go centre ..	8 bars

C.   *Fantasiestücke.* No. 3.   *Their Quarrel*

Play 16 bars. Cut 32 bars. Play to end (8 bars)

Pierrot Noir : ' You here ? Why ? '	2 bars
Pierrot Blanc : ' You here ? Why ? '	2 bars
Pierrot Noir : ' You go away '	2 bars
Pierrot Blanc : ' I stay here '	2 bars
Both Pierrots : ' We stay here. Why ? '	4 bars
Both Pierrots : ' She walks up and down ' ..	4 bars
Pierrot Noir : ' I have poem '	2 bars
Pierrot Blanc : ' I have flowers '	2 bars
Both Pierrots : ' I adore her '	4 bars

D.   *My Ladye's Minuet.*   *The Marquise and the Girls*

Play 42 bars. Cut 16 bars. Play to end (45 bars)

Introduction. Pierrots to corners	2 bars
Entrance of Servant	8 bars
Entrance of Marquise and Girls. Sit	12 bars
Pierrots up to back	15 bars

Marquise speaks (*a*) to Girls	5 bars
(*b*) to Servant	6 bars
Servant to Girls with ribbon	8 bars
First Girl makes cat's-cradle (Pierrots behind Servant)	4 bars
Second Girl takes it	4 bars
First Girl takes it and Second Girl muddles it ..	8 bars
First Girl up and run off	4 bars
Second Girl up and run off	4 bars
Servant bows and off	7 bars

E. *Nachtstücke.* No. 4.   *The Pierrot's Declaration*

Play straight through

Pierrots to up left—Blanc in front	2 bars
Walk towards Marquise—Blanc in front—and back to corner, changing places	4 bars
Walk towards Marquise—Noir in front. Blanc pulls Noir back and steps in front	4 bars
Blanc speaks. Noir to down left	4 bars
Noir speaks. Both to centre	4 bars
Both : ' I love you.' Meet centre	4 bars
Marquise between them—round left and back to centre. Pierrots following ; finish Blanc down right. Noir down left	11 bars
Both : ' I love you.' Kneel, offering gifts	4 bars
She takes them. Picture. Hush ! She sits. Pierrots behind seat	8 bars

F. *My Ladye's Minuet.*   *Monsieur le Marquis*

Play 42 bars. Cut 16 bars. Play to end (45 bars)

Introduction	2 bars
Entrance of Servant	8 bars
Servant : ' M'sieu from there to here is coming.' Bow	12 bars
Pierrots heads up. Extinguish each other ..	8 bars
Marquise puts roses in Pierrots' gifts	18 bars
Entrance of Marquis and Girls	8 bars
Marquis speaks and gives necklace	8 bars
Gives ring	8 bars
Says : ' You and I into the house,' and gives hand	4 bars
Exeunt Marquis, Marquise, Servant, Girls to down	

centre and say, ' Married ! '' Pierrots up and
say, ' Married ! ' ..   .. 11 bars

G.   *Nachtstücke*. No. 1.   *The Pierrots' Despair*

        Play 24 bars. Cut to end

Pierrot Blanc away to centre. Noir, head on arms   8 bars
Pierrot Blanc takes flowers and goes centre   ..   4 bars
Pierrot Noir takes poem and goes down right   ..   4 bars
Both turn. Noir goes up to centre. Embrace   ..   4 bars
Sob   ..   ..   4 bars

H.   *Nachtstücke*. No. 4.   *The Pierrots' Joy*

        Play 10 bars. Cut to end

Both see flowers. Break away   ..   ..   ..   2 bars
Take out flower. Kiss it   ..   ..   4 bars
Pierrot Blanc round left and to up centre. Noir to
    down right   ..   ..   2 bars
Both say : ' She loves me ! ' Picture   ..   ..   2 bars

COSTUME

Period : Eighteenth Century

Pierrot Blanc :

White Pierrot suit, loose trousers and coat, edged with narrow
    band of green. Green pom-poms.
White ruff.
White stockings.
White shoes, heeled and buckled.
White skull-cap.
White make-up.

Pierrot Noir :

Black Pierrot suit, trimmed green as above.
Black ruff.
Black stockings.
Black shoes.
Black skull-cap.
White make-up.

Madame la Marquise :

Buckle shoes.
White silk stockings.
Panniers.

Silk or brocade dress, with low, square-cut neck and sleeves to just below the elbow, finished with lace.

Hair : White wig dressed low on the top, or own hair. Small wreath of roses fixed at the side.

Monsieur le Marquis :

Black buckle shoes with red heels.

White silk stockings.

Satin knee-breeches.

Skirted coat, in satin or brocade.

Embroidered waistcoat.

Lace jabot.

Lace ruffles at the wrist.

White or grey powdered wig, the queue tied with black *moiré* ribbon.

Jeunes Filles :

Flat shoes, rose-coloured.

White silk stockings.

Eighteenth-century ballet dresses, with short sleeves, fitting bodices, outlined at neck with flowers, one pale pink, one pale blue.

Full petticoats (tarlatan). Small flower-wreath on the hair, which is smoothly dressed and unpowdered.

Negro Servant :

Baggy red or blue trousers.

Dull gold tunic coat, sleeveless, over yellow shirt. Emerald green waist-binding, with long ends edged with gold fringe.

Red Eastern shoes.

Yellow turban.

Black make-up.

PROPERTY PLOT

Stage :

Rostrum in opening centre back.

3 tread steps.

Ditto off stage up right.

Stone garden seat.

Curtain set, or tree-cloth at back.

Sky cloth, lit night-blue.

Hand :

Book	.. ..	*Marquis*
Two red roses	.. ..	*Marquise*
Sheaf of lilies	.. ..	*Pierrot Blanc*
Scroll of poem	.. ..	*Pierrot Noir*
Silver tray	.. ..	*Servant*
Length of narrow scarlet ribbon	.. ..	*Ditto*
Diamond necklace in case	.. .. ..	*Marquis*
Diamond ring	.. ..	*Ditto*

THE MARRIAGE OF COLUMBINE

(Music selected from works by Leonard Butler and Alec Rowley.)

The play has been performed at The Arts Theatre, London, July 1928, and has formed part of the examination plays performed by students of the Central School of Speech Training and Dramatic Art, London, for the Diploma in Dramatic Art of the University of London. It has also formed part of the programmes of Ginner-Mawer Company performances in Hyde Park, under the auspices of the League of Arts. The play was on all occasions produced by the author.

THE MARRIAGE OF COLUMBINE

It is the day of Columbine's wedding, and as she is the love of all the town, all the town is there to see. Columbine is marrying Scaramouche. 'How fortunate,' sigh all the girl friends. 'How desperate,' sigh all her rejected suitors. 'How ravishing she looks,' say all the bridesmaids. 'How exquisitely pretty the bridesmaids are,' say all the groomsmen. Columbine says nothing, but the tears still lingering in her pretty eyes speak for her. Pierrot says, 'I shall die'; Harlequin says, 'Nonsense, I shall marry her myself.'

The time is Victorian, when weddings were so fine, and everybody had so many relations. They all came to the wedding, so the company consists of:

Columbine ..	..	..	*A Bride*
Her Father ..	..	..	*A Man of Property*
Her Mother ..	..	..	*A Perfect Lady*
Scaramouche ..	..	..	*A Bridegroom with more Wealth than Beauty.*

Harlequin
Pierrot
Bridesmaids
Groomsmen
Columbine's Girl Friends
Rejected Suitors
Friends of the Family, and—
    other Relations.

The scene is laid outside the Church. Up right are steps leading into the Church.

A.   The curtain rises on an empty scene; then there enter three of Columbine's girl friends, all a-twitter with excitement. They make a group centre, and chatter together.

First Girl : ' She is to be married ! '

Second Girl : ' And he has money in piles and piles ; like this ! '

Third Girl : ' Oh, but her dress is so exquisite ! '

And they all sigh in ecstasy at the remembrance of a glimpse of Columbine dressed for her wedding. And there are other things—frilly, lacy things—only to be mentioned in whispers ; and three little heads are placed close together, inside three large bonnets, while three small pairs of feet can hardly keep still below three frilly crinolines.

But the sounds of the wedding cortège are heard approaching, and the girls break away, up stage right, determined to have the best view of everything.

B.   The sounds of the wedding procession draw nearer. And there enter the lady and gentlemen friends of the family in couples and little groups, preceded by the first lady and gentlemen, who move to the centre, discussing their own clothes and other people's. The men, conscious of extra high collars, flowered waistcoats just a shade tighter than is comfortable, of high hats a little too small in the head, carnations in buttonholes, and yellow gloves with elusive buttons ; the ladies conscious of their own toilet well performed, but suspicious of each other's billowing perfections. Every one is a little strained, but expectant.

The first lady speaks to her husband : ' She is to be married.'

He replies : ' The fellow has money, I hear. Quite satisfactory.'

Two of Columbine's rejected lovers have joined the crowd. There is despair in their whiskers and high black hats, despair in their very boots and gloves.

First Suitor : ' She is to be married ! '

Second Suitor : 'He is fat ! '

Both : ' We are very depressed. Ah ! How exquisite she is ! '

Now, from down right and left come the immortal lovers of Columbine, Harlequin and Pierrot. In spite of the very Victorian costumes of the other guests they keep their

GIRL FRIENDS OF THE BRIDE
IN 'THE MARRIAGE OF COLUMBINE'
From 'Modes de Paris,' 1838

traditional clothes; Harlequin, the eternally successful lover, long, slim and graceful, always smiling behind his black half-mask, always half dancing with his long spangled legs, a red rose pinned to his sweeping black cloak, and his wand at his side to show he is still Mercury, the Messenger of the Gods. He has a coil of rope over one arm.

Pierrot is the poet-lover, always a-dream when action is required, with his white face matching his white suit, and his long, white hands a-droop, or feeling for his poem or his pen. They meet down centre, back to back, but, being absorbed each in his own reflections, do not notice each other.

Pierrot, very depressed : ' She is to be married ! I shall die at her feet ! '

Harlequin : ' Personally, I shall marry her myself.'

They are lost in the crowd, which bustles about the stage, exchanging gossip, and every one hoping to find the best position from which to see the arrival of the bride.

At last she comes, all veiled and rather downcast, leaning on her father's arm. She might be any little Victorian bride, followed by her bridesmaids, with their stiff posies of flowers, but *we* know that she is Columbine, because her little wings are showing between her shoulders, and we feel that at any moment she might fly away once more to Mount Olympus. Her mother follows with her handkerchief held to her eyes in a very genteel manner.

Alone, and in splendid raiment, which includes a large cloak and plumed hat that he must have brought from Italy long years ago, comes Scaramouche. He looks like an ordinary man of wealth, if a little odd in dress, save that the size of his nose and stomach are strangely reminiscent of masks and carnivals. He is followed by the groomsmen, immaculate young gentlemen with peg-top trousers and side-whiskers.

When all the company is collected, Columbine's father pompously announces that his daughter is about to wed Scaramouche. He joins their hands, and bids the guests proceed into the church. They do so, rustling expensively and saying once more : ' The sweet child. Such a good match ' ; ' I hardly care for green feathers myself,' etc., etc.

Scaramouche precedes them, a very affable bridegroom—not young perhaps, but his watch-chain testifies to his highly satisfactory bank balance.

Columbine's mother and father turn up stage, chatting with their guests, and linger a moment at the foot of the steps, back to audience, to wrestle with a particularly evasive button of father's right glove. The bridesmaids kneel behind the bride, adjusting the flowers on the train of her dress. Columbine, very agitated behind her veil, remains practically alone for a moment with her two lovers, Harlequin and Pierrot.

C.   Pierrot approaches her very diffidently and sorrowfully, and says : ' Do lift your veil.'

Timidly she raises it, and looks at him. At the sight of her dear little tear-stained face Pierrot falls on his knees, and kisses the hem of her dress. What else can he do, he is so poor ? But he offers her his last poem, ' Ode to an Angel being Married.' She kisses it and hides it in her dress, almost crying for the sorrow of poor gentle Pierrot, who has loved her so faithfully. Pierrot turns away. She is lost to him.

D.   Then Harlequin, still gallant and smiling, approaches from the other side. She daren't look at him. He does make her heart flutter so. But somehow one of her hands is in his, and—and—he is kissing it. And :

' Columbine,' he says, ' I love you.'

Her heart flutters so terribly. What *is* to be done ? She never can resist him when he talks like that. Her hands try to still the little beating heart. She knows she will look at him in a moment. She had better swoon.

She swoons, into the arms of the bewildered and tearful bridesmaids.

Pierrot is aghast. Harlequin turns away with a strangely confident smile—perhaps he had seen a lady swoon before. Columbine's father and mother turn, horrified to find their child unconscious, almost at the altar-steps. Father fumes, and, extracting, with considerable difficulty, a large bandana handkerchief from a pocket in the tails of his coat, fans

Columbine's face, purple himself with anxiety, heat, rage, and unaccustomedly tight garments. Mother takes Columbine's limp hand and pats it agitatedly, wishing she had brought the smelling-salts.

Harlequin approaches Father as the latter turns away hopelessly from his child, who, as usual, is upsetting all his plans at the last moment.

Harlequin : ' Sir, will you permit me ? I think I have a remedy.'

Father : ' Oh ! Anything you like, my dear fellow. I wash my hands of these d—— women, and their swoonings and what-nots.'

Harlequin takes the rose from his cloak, and, slipping into it a note he has prepared, places the rose beneath Columbine's nose. Her mother is now weeping into her handkerchief, and so does not notice that her daughter opens her eyes suspiciously suddenly at that well-known scent. Harlequin whispers : ' Hush,' and points to the concealed note. Columbine looks at it. Smiles, and nods, ' I understand.' Then she slowly and deliberately rises to her feet, the perfectly composed little bride. Perhaps the bridesmaids saw, but Harlequin is such a dear, and their darling Columbine is smiling serenely once more. So who cares ? Not they, the little minxes.

E.   Now father pulls out his watch. They are gerting late as usual. Columbine has recovered ? Thank heaven for that. These women—well—well. Columbine passes into church with her bridesmaids and her parents. But on the top step she manages to turn and give Harlequin a little wave of the hand, and Harlequin, now in the centre of the stage, throws a thousand kisses after the demurest little bride who ever wore orange-blossom.

When Columbine looks like that, and Harlequin starts throwing kisses, you may be sure something is going to happen.

F.   Of course Harlequin has a plan. He calls to Pierrot, who joins him. ' These cords,' he says, ' are to bind the old man in there.'

' Oh,' says Pierrot, mystified but hopeful.

' But first,' says Harlequin, ' he must be brought out here.'

' Oh,' says Pierrot again.

' I have it,' says Harlequin, ' you take this note to him.'

' I see,' says Pierrot, light dawning on his rather slow intelligence.

Harlequin takes him by the shoulders, and, like conspirators, they approach the church door, and Harlequin pushes him in. While he is alone, Harlequin hides beside the church door, and gets ready his bat. Scaramouche comes out, pompously, to inquire who dares to send for him at the very moment when he is about to be married. Harlequin leaps upon him from behind, fells him with his bat, and gags him. But first he has whipped off his cloak and hat. Now Pierrot brings the cords and helps to bind Scaramouche. Before the astonished little fat man has realized what has happened, they have rolled him away into a corner, left, and Harlequin orders Pierrot to sit on his chest. This he does with relish, and at once begins to write a triumphant ' Ode on the Defeat of an Enemy.' While he is so engaged, Harlequin whips a false nose from his pocket, puts on Scaramouche's hat and cloak, and departs pompously into the church to take the place of the now prostrate bridegroom. Pierrot realizes the full meaning of the plot too late, but rushes in after him.

G.   Gagged and bound Scaramouche lies, near to explosion with rage and injured dignity, while, from the church, come sounds of the Marriage Service in progress. Scaramouche struggles to a sitting position, but as the Wedding March is heard, he falls back, purple in the face.

H.   Now the church doors open, and the guests, bridesmaids, and groomsmen pour out, chattering about the brilliant event, all anxious to see the happy pair come out of church. When, crash ! Before their horrified gaze there rolls a dishevelled form. Can this be Scaramouche, the wealthy, the affable bridegroom ? It is. . . . Panic ensues.

THE BRIDE'S MOTHER
IN 'THE MARRIAGE OF COLUMBINE'
From 'Modes de Paris,' 1838

I.   The bridesmaids faint into the arms of the groomsmen. The little minxes, as if they hadn't known all the time ! The ladies rush forward, and bend over the still-writhing Scaramouche. They fling their hands to heaven and retreat hastily. Such language ! The men advance towards him, but the ladies call them back, and everybody moves in an agitated circle round the still prostrate form ; of course nobody *does* anything. Father and mother appear on the church steps. The crowd gives way and points to what lies on the ground. ' Here is the bridegroom ! '

Father advances, and says, ' Untie him, some one,' and a good deal more as well. Mother weeps. The crowd is distraught, as a fuming Scaramouche, free at last, staggers to his feet, demanding immediate satisfaction from some one. And, upon the top of the steps appear, smiling, radiant, a very newly married Columbine and her bridegroom, Harlequin.

J.   Amid the general consternation the newly wedded lovers humbly approach Columbine's father and beg for his forgiveness. It is easy to be humble when the game is won. They have no arguments in their favour, save their youth.

Father is not impressed. He is, indeed, very angry, and not at all sure that he has not been made a fool of ; uncertain whether she is pleased or distressed, mother once more takes refuge in genteel tears.

But Scaramouche, thirsting for revenge of some kind, catches sight of Pierrot. ' Ah, it was he who brought the false message. He is the root of all the trouble.'

Scaramouche makes for the unfortunate Pierrot, who, though sad that he yet again has lost his Columbine, is, for once, quick enough, and dodges away among the crowd and out of sight, down right, Scaramouche panting after him.

Harlequin and Columbine together make the ever-simple, indisputable remarks, ' I love him ' and ' I love her.'

With the departure of the enraged ex-bridegroom a gloom is lifted from the assembly. After all, Harlequin is obviously so much better suited to Columbine than the unattractive Scaramouche.

Father realizes that nothing can be done, and so decides to be magnanimous. ' Let us avoid a scandal at all costs.' He lays his hands in blessing upon the two culprits still kneeling before him.

Harlequin raises his blushing little bride. He kisses her before them all. Who could resist kissing Columbine as a bride ?

K. The wedding procession forms once more, and, amid showers of rose-leaves and confetti, Harlequin leads Columbine away to the wedding breakfast.

As the last guests are disappearing, Pierrot, still running, rushes across the front of the stage, pursued by a panting Scaramouche. As usual Pierrot is the scapegoat for Harlequin's pranks. But Columbine still carries his poem near her happy little heart.

NOTES ON MUSIC

Music required :

Village Reminiscences	Leonard Butler
(Published by Augener & Co., Ltd.)	
Valentines	Leonard Butler
(Published by Lengnick.)	
An Ayre and March	Jeremiah Clarke
	(arr. by Alec Rowley)
(Published by Winthrop Rogers.)	

A. *Village Reminiscences :* ' High in the Belfry ' .. Butler
       Entrance of Columbine and Girl Friends

Introduction	8 bars
Entrance of girls	8 bars
First girl : ' She is to marry him '	8 bars
Second girl : ' He has money in piles and piles ' ..	8 bars
Third girl : ' Her dress and veil are exquisite ' ..	8 bars
All run to centre	8 bars
They lead round into a diagonal line right ..	8 bars

B. *March.* .. .. Clarke
    Entrance of Friends, Bridal Procession, Pierrot and
               Harlequin

Introduction	8 bars

Entrance of ladies and gentlemen. First couple move to centre	4 bars
First lady : ' She is to be married '	4 bars
First gentlemen : ' He has plenty of money ' ..	4 bars
Entrance of rejected suitors	4 bars
They say : ' She is to be married.' ' He is fat.' ' I shall die.'	8 bars
General movement	12 bars
Entrance of Harlequin and Pierrot	4 bars
Pierrot : ' She is to be married. I shall die.' ..	4 bars
Harlequin : ' I shall marry her myself.'	4 bars
Entrance of bride, her father and mother, brides-maids and bridegroom	8 bars
Father joins the hands of Scaramouche and Columbine	4 bars
The guests, followed by Scaramouche, go into church	11 bars

C.   *Valentines*. No. 1. .. .. Butler

Play 17 bars

Pierrot and Columbine

Pierrot crosses to Columbine	5 bars
Pierrot : ' You lift your veil.' She does so ; he kneels	4 bars
He kisses her dress and gives her a poem ..	4 bars
She looks at it and puts it in her dress	4 bars

D.   *Valentines*. No. 7. .. .. Butler

Harlequin and Columbine

Harlequin crosses to Columbine	5 bars
He kisses her hand and says : ' I love you.' ..	8 bars
Columbine faints	4 bars
Father and mother come down to Columbine ..	8 bars
Father fans her with his handkerchief. Mother pats her hand	8 bars
Harlequin goes to father	5 bars
Harlequin : ' Can I do anything ? ' Father : ' Yes, do, do ! '	4 bars
Harlequin goes to Columbine and gives her the rose. She opens her eyes	4 bars
Harlequin says : ' Hush ! ' Columbine reads the note, stands up and all hold the picture ..	8 bars

E.   *March.*   ..   ..   Clarke
Last 11 bars only
Columbine and Bridesmaids into Church

F.   *Village Reminiscences.* Madrigal.   ..   ..   ..   Butler
The Plot

Harlequin fetches cords	4 bars
Harlequin calls Pierrot to centre	4 bars
Harlequin says : ' These cords to bind him, but first he must come here '	8 bars
Harlequin gives note to Pierrot and both turn ..	9 bars
Pierrot and Harlequin move up to steps ; Pierrot exits	4 bars

On Repeat :

Harlequin prepares rope, hat and gag, and goes up right centre	8 bars
Enter Scaramouche ; Harlequin strikes him ..	4 bars
They bind Scaramouche	4 bars
Roll him to left	4 bars
Pierrot sits on him. Harlequin puts on cloak and hat	5 bars
Harlequin exit into church followed by Pierrot ..	4 bars

G.   *Wedding March.*   ..   ..   Mendelssohn
Play 8 bars
Scaramouche struggles to sitting position and falls back

H.   *March.*   ..   ..   Clarke
First 20 bars followed by roll in bass
Guests out of Church
On roll Scaramouche rolls into centre

I.   *Village Reminiscences.* ' The Carrier's Song '   ..   Butler
General Consternation of Guests

Ladies into centre and out	4 bars
Men into centre and out	4 bars
All round in circle to left	4 bars
All round in circle to right	4 bars
Father and mother appear on steps ; move down. Father says : ' Untie him '	4 bars

THE GUESTS
IN 'THE MARRIAGE OF COLUMBINE
From 'Modes de Paris,' 1838

Scaramouche up	.. ..	4 bars
Harlequin and Columbine appear on steps	..	4 bars

J.   *Ayre.*   .. .. Clarke

Columbine and Harlequin pray for Forgiveness

Harlequin and Columbine to father	.. ..	4 bars
They kneel	.. ..	4 bars
Scaramouche sees Pierrot and chases him off	..	4 bars
Harlequin and Columbine speak together ..	..	2 bars
Father blesses them ; they get up ..	.. ..	6 bars
They come down centre and turn towards exit	..	5 bars

K.   *March.*   .. .. Clarke

Last 23 bars only

Exit Harlequin and Columbine followed by father, mother and crowd	.. ..	16 bars
Scaramouche chases Pierrot across the front	..	7 bars

COSTUME

Period : 1838

Columbine :

Wedding dress in white muslin or organdie, with fitting bodice, off the shoulders.

Short sleeves, frilled, to elbow.

Orange blossom.

Large crinoline hoop.

Veil with wreath of orange blossom.

White three-quarter-length gloves.

Small circular bouquet.

White stockings.

Flat black sandal shoes.

Bridesmaids :

Dresses in muslin or organdie, white with dotted or lined pattern.

Fitting bodices, off the shoulders, with short sleeves, frilled, to the elbow.

Flounced skirts to the ground.

Large crinoline hoops.

Sandal shoes.

White stockings.
Three-quarter-length gloves.
Bouquets.
Hair : In knot or rolls at the back, with curls hanging on
each side of the face.
Spray or wreath of roses.

Columbine's Mother :

Purple or green shot silk gown over large crinoline. Fitting
bodice with long sleeves.
Green dolman, or embroidered shawl.
Poke bonnet (well back on the head) in lavender silk, with
curtain veil at the back ; sprays of flowers on and inside
the brim.
Fawn or coloured gloves.
White stockings.
Black sandal shoes.

Girl Friends :

Crinoline dresses in silk or muslin, in pale shades. Fitting
bodices with low necks, elbow sleeves.
Poke bonnets.
Shawls optional.

Lady Guests :

As illustration, or other dresses of the period, with bonnets
and shawls.

(For all above costumes see illustrations.)

Harlequin :

Spangled Harlequin suit.
Black skull-cap.
Ruffle.
Cloak.
White stockings.
Sandal shoes.
Harlequin bat.

Pierrot :

White Pierrot suit, with loose coat, trousers, ruffle.
Black or white skull-cap.
White shoes and stockings.

Bride's Father, Rejected Suitors, Groomsmen :

Men's costumes for 1838.
Tight-fitting trousers in buff or grey, strapped under patent-
leather boots or shoes.
Flowered satin double-breasted waistcoats.
Tail coats in brown or dark blue.
Stock collars with broad ties.
Lavender or yellow gloves.
Top-hats.
Side whiskers.
Wigs.

Scaramouche :

As above, with large black cloak and wide-brimmed black
felt hat.
Gold fob or watch-chain.
Rings.

PROPERTY PLOT

Stage :

Rostrum.
3 tread steps.
Dark backing behind rostrum.
Steps leading off rostrum, off stage.
Curtain set.

Hand :

Coil of rope	*Harlequin*
Rose	*Ditto*
2 pieces of paper	*Harlequin*
Quill pen and 2 pieces of paper..	*Pierrot*
Watch	*Father*
Bandana Handkerchief ..	*Ditto*
Handkerchief	*Mother*
Gag	*Harlequin*

PIERROT'S GARDEN

(Music selected from ' L'Almanach aux Images '
by Gabriel Grovlez.)

The play has been performed at the Albert Hall Theatre, forming part of a lecture-demonstration to the Summer School of the Central School of Speech Training and Dramatic Art, 1931.

CAST :

Pierrot	..	..	..	*Joyce Ruscoe.*
His Wife	..	..	..	*Irene Mawer.*

Produced by the author.

PIERROT'S GARDEN

Pierrot has a garden. That is partly because he is married, and partly because he likes flowers. If you are married you need to feel a Man of Property, and if you love Columbine, you are almost sure to like flowers, because she does. So Pierrot has a garden ; it is not a large garden, it consists of a pleasant green tub full of earth ; at present, it contains nothing else, but this play is concerned with the remedying of that. As Pierrot is a gardener, of course he also owns a trowel and a watering-can. He is newly married, and consequently rather excited and important, and the persons of the play are just simply

      Pierrot and
      His Wife, who was Columbine, but who has now
        settled, she hopes, into domesticity.

The Scene is an open space outside Pierrot's house. Down right stands the pleasant green tub of earth, with a stick in it to help to train the flowers when they begin to grow, while, up right, are arranged, neatly, Pierrot's trowel and watering-can.

It is a bright and sunny morning, the birds are busy, and it's just the sort of weather that makes even the most lugubrious gardener say, ' Grand growin' weather ! '

A.   Pierrot evidently feels the same. For he enters with jaunty step from up left, carrying, with great care, in the palm of his left hand, a large, important-looking seed. He holds up the seed in his right hand so that we can see it, then puts it back and says, ' I shall plant my seed, and then it will grow into a great big flowering-tree.' Enchanted with the idea, he lays the seed carefully on the ground, walks with deliciously important and excited steps up right, and returns with his trowel. He kneels beside the tub and prepares to dig a hole, when . . . !

    Horror ! He sees a large and wriggling worm ! But dangers must be faced—no real gardener is afraid of a worm.

So very cautiously he picks it up between finger and thumb. It wriggles horribly, and he nearly drops it, when, from a tree on his left, a bird chirps suddenly and hungrily. Much relieved to be rid of the responsibility, Pierrot throws away the worm and tells the bird to come and fetch it.

Now he returns to the important business of digging a hole for his seed. This done, he picks up the seed, places it carefully in the hole, pats down the earth over it—and sits back on his heels to await events. He is rather hazy as to how long a seed will take to grow, as he is new to gardening, but he supposes it cannot be long before the first shoot appears. He is doomed to disappointment; nothing happens at all. Gardening is dull work.

Then suddenly a bright idea occurs to him. One waters things when they are first planted, of course; how foolish of him to forget.

Happily excited by his great idea, Pierrot trots up right once more and returns with his watering-can.

He waters the seed, puts down the can, and again watches anxiously. But—nothing appears. He stands sulkily beside his empty garden, the disappointed artist.

B.   Now his wife appears from the house. She never can stay indoors doing the housework when the sun is shining. She looks cautiously to see if Pierrot is there, and then, all Columbine, and very little married woman, she flies towards him, only to be greeted with a most unpromising-looking back. ' Dear, dear, dear, *now* what's upset him ? ' she wonders, and, once more the helpful little wife, she approaches him, taps him on the shoulder and says, ' What is the matter, my dear ? '

Pierrot turns to her, points tragically to the seed, and says, ' Damn thing won't *grow* ! '

' Oh, poor Pierrot,' says the little wife, patting his head, consolingly. As she does so, she notices a spray of roses tucked into her dress, and she has her Great Idea.

She leads Pierrot up to the back and tells him to hide his eyes, turning him round with his back to the tub as she does so. He obediently covers his eyes with his hands.

Columbine flies down to the tub, takes the roses from her dress, and fixes them on to the stick which is in the tub, smiling a half-motherly smile as she does so. ' They are easy to manage, these men-children ! ' Then she floats back to Pierrot, turns him round so that he is facing the tub, takes his hands away from his eyes, and standing on tiptoe behind him, blindfolds him with her own.

Together they walk down towards the tub, he blinded and she pushing him. They arrive. She takes away her hands and says, ' Look there ! ' And, behold, his seed has grown (as he always knew it would) into a beautiful little rose-tree with red roses on it. He is not exactly proud. Gardens are like that, if you only know just how to do it.

He must show it to Columbine properly. No mere just running into a thing ; a new rose-tree must be approached with suitable solemnity.

C.   Pierrot springs back to the entrance, offers his arm to Columbine, suggesting that they shall take a stroll round the garden. She is beside him in a moment, her arm in his, the dutiful little wife prepared to admire her lord's domain.

They circle the stage. Pierrot points out the best bits as they pass. Here is the herbaceous border, there are the fruit-trees. She nods, and is duly impressed—they have played the game before.

Then, taken quite by surprise, they arrive at the rose-garden. Pierrot draws her attention to the beautifully-flowering rose-bush. ' A mere trifle, of course, but my own planting.'

Columbine is enchanted. 'How delicious the flowers must smell. Clever Pierrot to grow such a splendid rose-garden ! '

Pierrot's heart stirs. How he loves Columbine—everything he has is hers. He will even pick his rose for her. And splendidly he does so.

Gallantly, he kneels before her, just as he used to do when they were courting. He holds out his precious rose to her, and bends his head for the touch of her hands upon it in blessing.

Perhaps it was lucky that he bent his head just at that

moment. Otherwise even a man could hardly have failed to see that the look she gave him, as she replaced the flowers in her dress in the exact spot from which she had taken them a few moments before, was more motherly than wifely. What she *said* to him was, ' Oh, Pierrot, how good of you to give me your beautiful rose that you grew yourself.' But what she *thought* was, ' Oh, I'm so glad he's never grown up.'

They look very happy in Pierrot's garden as the curtains close upon them.

NOTES ON MUSIC

Music Required :

L'Almanach aux Images .. .. Gabriel Grovlez
(Published by Augener & Co., Ltd.)

A. Les Ânes. *Pierrot Plants His Seed*

Introduction	4 bars
Enter Pierrot to centre. Holds up and puts back seed	10 bars
' I plant the seed—it grows into big tree ' ..	8 bars
Puts down seed	4 bars
Up and fetch trowel ; back to centre and kneel ..	8 bars
Sees worm ; picks up ; throws away to bird ..	10 bars
Digs	9 bars
Plants seed	4 bars
Pats soil	4 bars
Watches seed ; disappointment	16 bars
Fetches watering-can..	8 bars
Waters ; looks, and nothing happens	5 bars

B. Chanson de l'Escarpolette. *Columbine joins Him*

Enter Columbine to Pierrot ; tap on shoulder ..	16 bars
Pierrot speaks : ' It won't grow '	3 bars
Columbine : ' Oh, poor Pierrot '	6 bars
Idea. Pierrot up stage. Tells him to hide eyes	14 bars
Columbine to tub ; puts flowers in	7 bars
Back to Pierrot ; puts her hands over eyes ..	8 bars
Back to tub ; uncovers eyes ; Pierrot sees flowers	10 bars

C.   *Les Ânes.*   *Pierrot Picks the Roses*

Last 32 bars

Both to entrance up left	3 bars
Walk round and to flower-pot	8 bars
Shows flower	8 bars
Pierrot picks flower, kneels and gives it ..	8 bars
She takes it. Picture	5 bars

PROPERTY PLOT

Curtain or garden set.

Stage :

Wooden tub full of earth, down right.

Trowel ⎫
Watering-can⎭ up right

Hand :

Large seed	*Pierrot*
Spray of red roses	*Columbine*

COSTUME

Pierrot :

Black or white Pierrot suit.

Skull-cap.

Ruffle.

Shoes (flat).

Stockings to match suit.

White make-up.

Columbine :

Full dress to ankles ; fitting bodice ; puff sleeves.

Crinoline.

White stockings.

Scarlet unblocked ballet shoes.

Hair : Dressed high at back, parted centre, side curls, bound with ribbon to match dress.

PRISCILLA, OR THE LOST COLUMBINE

(Music selected from the works of F. Rung, Jean Morel, Alex Roloff, and Moszkowski.)

This play was performed at the Scala Theatre, 1927, when the cast was as follows :

Priscilla	*Irene Mawer*
George, Her Husband	*John Laurie*
First Aunt	*Oonah Todd Naylor*
Second Aunt	*Doris Pillitz*
Clown	*Gwynneth Thurburn*
Pantaloon	*Dilys Harker*
Pierrot	*E. M. Thomas*
Harlequin	*Nina Silcock*

The play has also formed part of the Dramatic Examination performances of the Ginner-Mawer School, and of the Central School of Speech Training and Dramatic Art, for the Diploma in Dramatic Art, of the University of London.

It was, in each case, produced by the author.

PRISCILLA, OR THE LOST COLUMBINE

Once, hundreds of years ago, Columbine lived on Mount Olympus, but her name was Psyche then, and, like all the Dwellers on the Mountain, she was immortal. She wasn't called Columbine until she was travelling through Italy as a serving-maid in the Middle Ages. There she picked up her old friend Hermes,

TRADITIONAL COSTUMES OF CLOWN AND PANTALOON
SHOWING MAKE-UP IN 'PRISCILLA, OR THE LOST COLUMBINE'
(From 'Punch', 1855)

who became her lover Harlequin, living in Bergamo. And there she met Peppe Nappa and Piero, and of course they fell in love with her too, and then she also met Old Pantaleone. She met them all again later in France, where Pierrot spelled his name like that, and became a dreamer and a poet and loved Columbine more than ever, and so did Harlequin. Then they came to England, and Columbine was a dancing-girl. And there they all met their dear friend Joey the clown. And there, as this story tells, a very sad thing happened : Columbine got lost. It was her own fault, because she made a great mistake. But that didn't help matters. Her great mistake was that she got married, a dangerous thing for Columbine to do in any case, but in this case she married the wrong man. At least so her friends said. But she wasn't quite sure about it herself. George, her husband, was certainly ' very Victorian,' and, what was worse, he had two completely Victorian aunts who lived with him even after he was married. And they didn't approve of Columbine (who was called Priscilla), because she couldn't leave off wanting to dance and would wear red ballet-shoes at all hours of the day.

Her friends were very distressed. They had never so completely lost Columbine before, and they determined to get her back again. So Clown and Pantaloon took service with George as butler and footman, and waited their opportunity to bring about a meeting between Priscilla and her old lovers, Pierrot and Harlequin, who meant to try and steal her back again to the Immortals, if only they could get at her, so the characters in the play are :

Priscilla   ..   *The Lost Columbine, now a prim little Victorian wife, whose feet* will *keep dancing*

George   ..   *Her husband, who is something successful in the City*

Two very Victorian Aunts

Clown   ..   ⎱ *Now Butler and Footman in Priscilla's*
Pantaloon   ⎰ *Home*

Harlequin

Pierrot

It is the day of Priscilla's birthday, and her friends have determined to make the attempt after supper of this day, when, most of all, little wives want to dance and to remember their immortal lovers. The scene is the dining-room of George's house in Bayswater. The table is set half-way up right, with four chairs beside it, one at each end, and two on the up stage side. There is a sideboard against the back wall, left of the centre entrance. The fireplace is down left, and placed diagonally before it is a sofa. The door of the room is up left. But there must be an invisible entrance in the curtains, centre, backed by a sky-cloth lit just like that moonlight night blue that always makes

*it so difficult for us to resist our dreams. It is evening. Just
before dinner-time. The room is lit brightly, but the fire also
gives a warm red glow from down left.*

A.   As the curtain rises the room is empty. But at once there
enters, from up left, the First Aunt. She sails in her crinoline
to up centre, and is joined there by her sister, the Second Aunt.
Together' they sail to the sofa by the fire, and at the same
moment sit upon it. Still moving simultaneously, they
produce two bags, and from them two mufflers and two sets
of knitting-needles, which for a moment they click indus-
triously. Then the First Aunt puts down her knitting, calls
her sister's attention to the fact that she is about to speak,
and speaks.

First Aunt : ' That child has been dancing again.'
Second Aunt : ' Yes, my dear, and showing her ankles.'
Both (with uplifted hands of horror) : ' Disgraceful ! '

B.   At this moment Priscilla runs in, her little red shoes
twinkling, her eyes alight, her arms full of flowers, and even
her prim lavender silk crinoline half suggestive of a remembrance of Columbine, with its little white apron and cherry-
coloured bows. Her arms are full of flowers, because it's her
birthday, and, mysteriously, these flowers have been left at
the door for her. She can't guess by whom, and if Clown and
Pantaloon know, they are silent. She runs joyously to down
stage centre, and for one moment we are allowed a glimpse
of the soul of Columbine inside her, and then, a moment later,
she is Priscilla, remembering to make her bobbing curtsies
to her husband's aunts.

But her attention is soon distracted from their disapproving
glances by the arrival of Clown and Pantaloon with the first
necessities for laying the supper. They have a queer, rolling,
tumbling gait for a butler and footman. Pantaloon is so
bandy-legged, and Clown can hardly restrain himself from
turning a somersault every moment. They run queerly across
to the table, and begin to lay the cloth as if it were one of
the best jokes in the world, and Priscilla joins them, placing
her flowers on the table for decoration. She chooses a

particularly sweet-smelling rose and lays it in George's place. He is a kind old thing, and she has always wanted him to love her, and it's her birthday, so she does want him to be good-tempered to-night ; but, oh dear ! you never know what sort of a day he may have had in the City, and it does make such a difference to his temper !

All her joyousness of soul is bubbling up inside her. She positively *must* kiss somebody, now this minute. And so, regardless of consequences, she runs across to the sofa, flings her arms round the neck of the astonished First Aunt, and, to that lady's horror, kisses her resoundingly. Will the child never learn manners !

But Priscilla, child indeed that she is, hears a little tune echoing in her head. She dreams a moment of dances she seemed to know in some other life. Then she floatingly dances a few steps down right, turns, and sees Clown. That worthy and Pantaloon have been watching her eagerly. The more Priscilla dances, the better their chance of recapturing Columbine. Clown now opens his arms in a ridiculous invitation, and Priscilla, flying into them, is whirled into an absurd waltz, until, whisking round a corner, the couple crash into the sofa, nearly upsetting the completely scandalized aunts.

Priscilla retreats hastily to the centre. ' Now there will be trouble,' she thinks. Clown is back beside Pantaloon, the perfect footman in a moment, standing stiffly to attention.

The aunts rise to their feet, pictures of outraged propriety. In no uncertain gesture they speak to Priscilla.

First Aunt : ' You are to dance no more.'

Second Aunt : ' And you are *not* to show your ankles.'

Priscilla is penitent. She is always trying to be good, but somehow her feet and her dreams *do* run away with her so. She stands a moment, half tearful. But then, like a grave child repeating a lesson she says : ' I am to dance no more.' And she nods her head firmly several times, as if really trying to remember. But all the same she can't help giving a little flick to her crinoline as she runs back to the table to see if all is ready. And then she hears the sound of George's latch-key.

' George,' say the aunts, ' he must hear of this.'

' The Master,' say Clown and Pantaloon, ' he *will* hear of this.'

' George,' says Priscilla, all in a flutter, ' I do hope he won't hear of this, because I do want him to have remembered my birthday.'

They say all that at once, and there's very little time for them to do more than think it, for now Priscilla is down stage right, smoothing her hair, as George always likes it tidy, and wondering if he will remember to kiss her.

C.   George enters to up centre. Priscilla, looking at him anxiously, fears it has *not* been a good day in the City. There is something forbidding about the side-whiskers protruding from his florid cheeks, and the very angle of the solid gold watch-chain upon his ample waistcoat portends trouble. However, she still hopes . . . It *is* her birthday, and she did look pretty when she peeped in the glass.

But George has handed his hat and stick to Clown and Pantaloon. He moves ponderously down centre, and laying a hand upon the upper region of his waistcoat bows cere-moniously to his aunts. Priscilla is all a-flutter, and looking so kissable—will he ? George looks at her, but does not move beyond the centre, where, advancing a somewhat forbidding whisker, he signifies, ' You may kiss me, Priscilla.' Very damped, poor little Priscilla walks solemnly up to him, lays her fingers on the back of his shoulders to steady herself, rises on tiptoe, and can just reach to plant a disappointed peck on his cheek. She retires again to her corner right, fearing trouble. And here it comes. For the aunts rise simultaneously.

' George,' says the First Aunt, ' listen to me.'

And, ' George,' says the Second Aunt, ' listen to me too.'

George prepares, testily, to listen.

First Aunt : ' That wife of yours has been dancing again.'

Second Aunt : ' And showing her ankles.'

Both : ' It really is disgraceful.'

George turns to the trembling Priscilla, who is already perilously near tears. She *knew* they'd spoil her birthday-party.

' Priscilla,' says George, in his hearthrug manner, ' Have you been dancing ? '

' Yes,' nods Priscilla, very quickly, a great many times, so that she shan't burst into tears.

' Well,' says George, as one who speaks for the last time, ' you are to dance *no more*.' And he turns away up left and folds his hands behind his back with complete finality.

Priscilla runs up to him beseechingly. He can't really mean it. But his immovable back, upon which might rest the whole of the British Constitution, is so relentless that she stamps a furious foot at it, and flounces away again, down left, not only near tears this time, but really crying.

D.   But now Clown and Pantaloon appear once more to save the situation. Still ridiculously waddling and dancing, they carry in the rest of the supper, with the dishes held high above their heads, because it's so much more fun to carry things like that than soberly in front of you. They lay the dishes on the table, advance to up stage centre, and with absurd gestures, made simultaneously, say, ' Ladies and gentlemen, the supper is served.'

E.   Priscilla pulls herself together, like the gallant little thing she is. Her supper-party shall be a success after all, with dear Clown and Pantaloon to help her. She runs across to the aunts, and, standing between them, takes a hand of each, and trips across the stage between them as they sail, galleon-wise, to the table. Then she looks at George, and sighs. It would have been fun if he'd offered her his arm, just this once, as it's her birthday, but he's still looking broody ! So she runs to him, and placing his hand in the middle of his chest for him, slips her hand into his arm, leads him to his place at the table, and seats herself beside him.

She watches him anxiously. Will he notice the flower she put there for him ? He *does* notice it, but, with a gesture of annoyance, throws it away as he unfolds his napkin. ' Really these servants are too careless, leaving things lying about like that ! '

Priscilla sighs. George really *isn't* very satisfactory as a lover. But perhaps she was wrong to expect it of a husband. But, somehow or other, she seemed to remember being *tremendously* loved once. But, like her dancing, this memory *can't* be quite nice, the aunts certainly wouldn't approve.

F.   George carves the rabbit pie rather ponderously. Priscilla always has rabbit pie on her birthday, and when they ask her why, she can only say, ' Joey always liked it so,' which never seems sense to anybody but Clown and Pantaloon. These worthies now hand the plates with due solemnity, and the party settles to supper.

G.   Now Clown sees his chance. He runs ridiculously to centre and beckons to Pantaloon to join him, and up waddles Pantaloon, wondering what Joey is up to now. Clown has an idea, which he expounds laboriously.
   ' You and I will give them some of that Vin d'Arlequin, and then *they* will fall asleep, and . . . well . . . see ? '
   Pantaloon is slow to pick up the idea, but he sees Clown's mouth opening prodigiously. It's evidently a joke. Vin d'Arlequin, the magic wine of the Immortals . . . they'll fall asleep. . . . Priscilla could be stolen away. . . . Ah ! He . . . he sees it. And off he goes into crows and cackles and side-splitting paroxysms of laughter with Clown.

H.   Then suddenly, with two simultaneous and ridiculous jumps, they turn, face the sideboard, run up to it, and pick up two bottles of wine. They run across to the table and pour out glasses for George and the two aunts, one of whom lays a forbidding hand on Priscilla's glass, signifying that she is too young for wine. Priscilla pouts. *She*, a married woman ; but Clown winks at her, and she half guesses a joke, while George and the aunts raise their glasses, drink a little, and replace the glasses on the table, with strange sighs of unusual contentment and well-being.

I.   Priscilla looks at them hopefully. Perhaps they will cheer up after all. But, to her amazement, their highly respectable heads begin to nod. Each in turn makes a heroic effort to

wake up, and looks reprovingly at the other heads sinking
swiftly into unconsciousness. But their efforts are unavailing,
and in a moment or two the scandal is complete—George and
his aunts are fast asleep at the supper-table.

Priscilla is near to tears again. Oh ! how dull they are.
But there is her little tune singing in her ears once more, so
she rises from the table, and rather sadly begins a few steps
of a dreamy dance.

But, oh ! It's so dull always dancing alone, and she breaks
off disconsolately. Clown and Pantaloon are watching and
listening eagerly. Will they come, Harlequin and Pierrot, her
immortal lovers, and steal back again the lonely Columbine
lost in a desert of respectability ? It's an anxious moment,
but their plot has succeeded well so far.

Priscilla is now sitting in a disconsolate heap, dreaming
by the fire.

J.   Surely ? Yes, the lights are turning blue for the moonlight of a dream, the curtains at the back are parted, and
there, waiting outside, is—Pierrot. Priscilla's figure, lit by
the warm glow of the fire, seems to shed its Victorian prim-
ness ; the flickering flames hide flowers in her hair, her face
and hands are like flowers too. Her eyes are starry. Once
more she is Columbine.

Pierrot stands a moment in the centre opening. He is all
that Pierrot should be—dreamy, poetical. In his hand he
holds his pen and book, and waits poised to catch the song
that is ever singing in his head. Then he sees Priscilla, and
all his love of long ago flows back to him. Priscilla, half
a-dream, rises from before the fire, and sees Pierrot. Her heart
gives just that flutter it always did when Pierrot made poems
for her in the moonlight in France in some other life. She flies
away down right, all a-flutter with excitement. Pierrot
follows her, and in a moment he is on his knees beside her,
and writing another verse to his immortal love song. Then
he speaks to her, saying :

' You are the lady of my poem——''

Priscilla is in more of a flutter than ever. She had always,
in secret, wanted George to write a poem for her. But George

only wrote cheques for the housekeeping, and there's no poetry in cheques.

Pierrot puts into her hand the poem he has written, and she reads it, thrilling at the words she had always longed to hear. Pierrot falls in a dream, however, at the sight of her flower-like hands touching his poem, and wanders away to the fire to compose a ' Sonnet to My Lady's Hands ', and promptly forgets all about Priscilla herself. Clown and Pantaloon are disappointed in him, but that's always the trouble with Pierrot, he does wander so terribly between inspiration and practicality.

K.   But what matter ? Here's Harlequin, all a-shimmer with silver spangles, smiling behind his black mask, gallant, irresistible. He sweeps down to Priscilla, where she stands as Pierrot left her, and she turns to find Harlequin bowing beside her. And Harlequin is such a disturbing person. Memories of Mount Olympus, thousands of years ago, of Italy, and of Drury Lane at Christmas-time seem to throng about her. Harlequin is kissing her hand. (And George had forgotten her birthday.) Now Harlequin gives her a lovely red rose, and everybody knows what *that* means. (And George threw away the one she gave him.)

Priscilla is all Columbine now. She floats away to centre with her love-gifts, Pierrot's poem, and Harlequin's rose, and stands with outstretched arms—a butterfly poised for flight, a little wife half-afraid, half-entranced, and the moonlight from somewhere or other touches her as it did in the old pantomime days of ' Limes '.

She can't see Harlequin, because she daren't look, but she can feel him drawing nearer and nearer. Then he is on his knees beside her, and saying, as only Harlequin *can* say it, ' I love you.'

At last Priscilla looks down at him and half-hesitatingly holds out her hand. But as he touches it she remembers Pierrot, dreaming by the fire. She slips away to him and touches him on the shoulder. He follows her as she runs back to Harlequin, and he falls on his knee on the other side of her. Hardly conscious of what she is doing, but radiant

4

with excitement, Priscilla holds out a hand to each, and as
the lovers bend to kiss the hands of Columbine, Clown and
Pantaloon steal up behind, and, unseen, extend their hands
in absurd benediction over the Immortal Lovers reunited in
Bayswater.

L.   But there's many a slip, and Columbine is not won back to
them yet. At the critical moment George gives vent to a
shattering and resounding sneeze. The dream is broken.
Pierrot and Harlequin fade into the shadows as the moonlight
gives place to the comfortable glow of a Bayswater dining-
room. Clown and Pantaloon are servants once more. George,
still only half-awakened, is wrestling with another threatening
sneeze. He has one of his colds. And Priscilla, bewildered
and rather conscience-stricken, wonders how she can have
dreamed so realistically as to be left with a tell-tale poem
and rose in her hands. She thrusts them hastily into her
dress and rushes to George. He needs careful management
when he has a cold ! At the moment he is ravaged by incipient
sneezes, and, handkerchief to nose, he gropes blindly towards
the sofa and the fire, led by Priscilla, all wifely solicitude.
He finally sinks upon the sofa as the culminating sneeze
explodes. There he sits the picture of suffering, the very
personification of a cold in the head. Priscilla in despera-
tion runs to the aunts and rouses them from the effects of
their sleep and implores their assistance.

M.   They rise to their feet and to the occasion. ' George has
a cold ; we have warned him so often about changing his
underwear so early in the Spring.'
    They sail down centre and regard the pitiable object he
presents, and tap their noses significantly. Priscilla, meanwhile, retreats down right and tries to collect her scattered
wits.
    The aunts, turning simultaneously, sail to the sideboard
and return to the sofa with cold-remedies. The First Aunt
stands behind George with a woollen muffler, the Second stands
centre with a large green bottle.
    The scarf is wound round and round the throat of the

protesting George, the bottle is thrust beneath his nose, but, after one sniff, he waves it weakly away. The aunts stand centre, and the First Aunt says, ' George, go upstairs to bed.'

George assents, and totters to centre between them, forming a little procession facing the door up left. George waves a hand, as if to say, ' Lead on ; it is a far, far better thing to go to bed.' The aunts sign to Priscilla to follow. Clown and Pantaloon miserably place candles in their hands as the aunts pass them, and the procession leaves the dining-room, and we hear George's last and most excruciating sneeze as he mounts the stairs. Priscilla stops centre, too bewildered to move. Her dream was so beautiful, and so suddenly shattered, she wonders if it can really have happened. Clown and Pantaloon look dejectedly round, wondering if there's any hope after all.

N. But now the light is turning to dreams and moonlight once more. And there is the little tune Pierrot and Columbine found in France : ' Au Claire de la Lune, mon ami Pierrot ' ; and as Priscilla feels for her rose and her poem, sure enough Harlequin and Pierrot steal out of the shadows again. This time Priscilla *dare* not look at them. She stands clasping her poem and her rose to her beating heart, with her eyes seeing, far, far down the centuries, all the dreams of love that have been hers. Harlequin and Pierrot are drawing nearer and nearer. Once more they kneel beside her. Once more Clown and Pantaloon creep up behind. Surely they have caught their Columbine after all. In another minute she must look at her lovers, and then she'll be away with them, far, far from marriage and Bayswater and George and cheques, when—George, in the distance, sneezes yet again, and the spell is broken.

But Priscilla has understood. The Immortals have called to Columbine, but she cannot go. She is held in Bayswater by something stronger than dreams and flowers. She is bound to George by wifely affection.

O. Yet for a moment she laughs as Columbine laughed of old, and tearing off one little red shoe, she flings it high into the air above the heads of Harlequin and Pierrot. Something of her is always theirs, she will never forget ; but as they catch the little red shoe of Columbine, Priscilla runs away to minister to the needs of her lawful husband George.

Harlequin and Pierrot slip into the moonlit opening, centre back, and raise aloft Priscilla's shoe, their memory of Columbine, where the moonlight haloes it with dreams. Clown springs to attention, a butler once more, and Pantaloon, unable to resist a joke, crawls under the table and peers from under the table-cloth at the closing scene. Clown can hardly resist saying, ' 'Ullo, old 'un,' to him, but refrains, as Priscilla appears once more.

P.   This time she leads George, swathed to the eyes in wraps and leaning on a stick, to the sofa by the fire. There she installs him comfortably. She knows he really enjoys a good ' fussing ' when he has a cold, and she *does* love to take care of somebody, and to be *needed*. Somehow the shadows of the firelit room are fraught with strange possibilities, and her one shoeless foot, which will protrude itself, has to be thrust beneath her crinoline. But the dreams are fading. The room is filled with the notes of the old song ' Home, Sweet Home ', and, after all, George is a dear old thing. Part of her will always live as Columbine with the Immortals ; there will always be a dance in her feet, but as she slips to the ground beside George, and he forgets his cold enough to find comfort in putting his arm about her, she realizes that in her heart Priscilla, the prim little wife, loves her perfectly Victorian husband.

The curtain falls on a picture that leaves Pantaloon shaking his head at the failure of their plot to recapture Columbine.

NOTES ON MUSIC

Music Required :

Menuet (from *Nordiska*, Book III)		F. Rung
Noah's Ark		A. Roloff
Moments Musicaux. Opus 84. No. 4 in G. ..		Moszkowski

(Published by Augener & Co., Ltd.)

A Dream Garden   ..   ..   J. Morel

(Published by Walsh & Co.)

Old Songs :   *Au Clair de la Lune*
            Home, Sweet Home

A.   *Menuet.*   F. Rung.   *Entrance of Aunts*

Play 16 bars and repeat them

Entrance of First Aunt	4 bars
Entrance of Second Aunt	4 bars
Both move down left and sit	8 bars

On Repeat :

They get out their knitting and knit	8 bars
First Aunt : ' She has been dancing '	4 bars
Second Aunt speaks : ' She has been showing her ankles '	4 bars

B.   *A Dream Garden.* No. 4. Morel.

Entrance of Priscilla, Clown, and Pantaloon

Entrance of Priscilla. She puts down her flowers and calls Clown and Pantaloon	16 bars
Entrance of Clown and Pantaloon	8 bars
Priscilla arranges her flowers, runs and kisses the First Aunt	8 bars
Priscilla begins to dance	8 bars
She goes to Clown, waltzes with him ; they bump into the sofa	8 bars
First Aunt speaks : ' You must not dance any more '	4 bars
Second Aunt speaks : ' You must not show your ankles '	4 bars
Priscilla speaks : ' I am not to dance ? Oh, very well ! '	8 bars
She finishes arranging the table and goes down right to wait for George. Clown and Pantaloon stand up centre	16 bars

C.   *Menuet.*   F. Rung.   *Entrance of George*

Begin at bar 17 ; play 20 bars. Play 8 bars and repeat them. Play 16 bars

Introduction	2 bars
Entrance of George; he bows to the Aunts ..	14 bars

Priscilla goes and kisses him .. .. .. 4 bars
First Aunt rises and says : ' Listen to me ' .. 4 bars
Second Aunt rises and says : ' Listen to me ' .. 4 bars

On Repeat :

First Aunt : ' She has been dancing again ' .. 4 bars
Second Aunt : ' She has been showing her ankles ' 4 bars
George : ' Have you been dancing ? ' .. .. 4 bars
Priscilla : ' Yes, I have ! ' .. .. 4 bars
George : ' You must not dance any more ' .. 4 bars
Priscilla crosses to George, stamps and runs down
right .. .. 4 bars

D. *Noah's Ark*. Roloff. ' The Elephant.' *The Supper*

Entrance of Clown and Pantaloon with the dishes 8 bars
They take off the covers and come to centre .. 4 bars
They say : ' Supper is served ! ' .. .. .. 4 bars

E. *Noah's Ark*. Roloff. ' The Cuckoo.' *The Supper (con.)*

Priscilla takes the Aunts to the table and they sit 12 bars
Priscilla takes George to the table and they sit 13 bars

F. *Noah's Ark*. Roloff. ' The Elephant.' *The Supper (con.)*

George carves the first plate .. .. .. 4 bars
George carves the second plate .. .. .. 4 bars
George carves the third plate .. .. .. 4 bars
George carves the fourth plate .. .. .. 4 bars

G. *Noah's Ark*. Roloff. ' The Lion.' *The Supper (con.)*

Clown comes to centre and calls Pantaloon .. 6 bars
Clown says : ' I will give them a drink, which will
send them to sleep ' .. .. 8 bars
They both laugh .. .. 4 bars

H. *Noah's Ark*. Roloff. ' The Tiger.' *The Supper (con.)*

Clown and Pantaloon turn .. .. .. 1 bar
They fetch the wine and pour it out .. .. 4 bars
The Aunts and George drink and begin to feel
drowsy .. .. 4 bars

I. *A Dream Garden*. No. 4. Morel.
Play 32 bars

Priscilla watches the family fall asleep and gets up   16 bars
She begins to dance, breaks off, and goes to the fire   16 bars

J.   *A Dream Garden.*   No. 2.   Morel.   *Pierrot*

           Play through and repeat

Entrance of Pierrot ..   ..   15 bars
Priscilla runs to down right. Pierrot follows and
     kneels   ..   ..   8 bars

On Repeat.

Pierrot says : ' I write a poem. You are the lady
     in my poem '   ..   ..   8 bars
He gives it to her   ..   ..   7 bars
She reads it and puts it in her dress. He wanders
     to the fire   ..   ..   8 bars

K.   *A Dream Garden.*   No. 1.   Morel.   *Harlequin*

Entrance of Harlequin. He bows to Priscilla   ..   8 bars
He kisses her hand and gives her a rose   ..   ..   8 bars
Columbine runs to centre, holding the rose and poem   16 bars
Harlequin kneels to her   ..   ..   4 bars
He says : ' I love you,' and kisses her hand   ..   8 bars
Priscilla fetches Pierrot They kneel one on each
     side of her. On the last chord George sneezes   8 bars

L.   *Menuet.*   F. Rung.   *George's Cold*

Begin at bar 37 ; play 8 bars and repeat them. Play 16 bars.
Pierrot and Harlequin run down right and left   ..   8 bars

On Repeat.

George sneezes again. Priscilla runs to him   ..   8 bars
He gets up and they go to the fire. On the last
     chord he sits on the sofa with another sneeze   16 bars

M.   *Moments Musicaux.*   No. 4.   Moszkowski.

       The Remedies and Exeunt Aunts and George

       Play 9 bars. Cut 6 bars. Play to end

The Aunts come down and look at George   ..   5 bars
They say to each other : ' He has a cold '   ..   4 bars
They fetch the bottle and the scarf   ..   ..   10 bars
First Aunt puts the scarf round his neck ..   ..   4 bars
Second Aunt puts the bottle under his nose   ..   4 bars

First Aunt says : ' George, go to bed '   ..   ..   2 bars
They form a procession and exeunt   ..   ..   10 bars

N.   *Au Clair de la Lune,*   *Priscilla's Dream Again*

16 bars

Pierrot and Harlequin come back. Clown and Pantaloon come down and stand behind Priscilla. On the last note George sneezes .. 16 bars

O.   *A Dream Garden.* No. 4. Morel. *Priscilla leaves the Immortals*

Play the last 16 bars

Priscilla takes off her shoe and throws it to Harlequin and Pierrot. They take it up centre. Priscilla runs off
Clown goes and stands by the sofa. Pantaloon goes under the table   ..   ..   16 bars

P.   *Home, Sweet Home.*

16 bars

Priscilla and George come back to the fire. George sits on the sofa and Priscilla on the floor beside him   ..   ..   16 bars

FURNITURE

Stage :

Victorian dining-table.
4 chairs.
Plush- or leather-covered sofa with a Paisley shawl or an antimacassar on the back of it.
Sideboard.

PROPERTY PLOT

On table, up right :

White cloth
4 wine-glasses.
2 chairs above table.
1 chair at right end of table.
1 chair at left end of table.

On Sideboard, up left :

2 wine-bottles.

2 candles in brass candlesticks.
Box of matches.
Medicine bottle.
Scarf.

Off Stage, left :

Hat		
Stick	.. ..	*George*
Dressing-gown		
2 workbags containing knitting		*Aunts*
Bouquet with one loose flower		*Priscilla*
Tray with 4 knives, 4 forks		*Clown*
Meat Pie under dish-cover		*Ditto*
Cruet		*Pantaloon*
4 plates		*Ditto*

Off Centre :

2 letters	*Pierrot*
Quill pen	*Ditto*
Rose	*Harlequin*

COSTUME

First and Second Aunts :

Crinoline of about 1864 (i.e. with a big hoop).

The bodice cut with a high neck and finished with a cream or white neckband.

Long, rather full, sleeves.

The whole dress carried out, one in black or black and white very small check taffeta or fine woollen material ; the other in plum colour or dark bottle green.

Paisley or black lace shawls may be worn.

Black cotton stockings.

Black flat-heeled shoes.

Hair : Either parted in the centre, or taken straight back off the forehead and plaited into a ' door-knocker ' and encased in a chenille net.

Priscilla :

Crinoline cut low in the neck and worn ' off ' the shoulders with short puff sleeves.

The bodice well boned and tight-fitting and cut to a point in
    front.

The dress carried out in a delicate colour in taffeta or heavy
    silk.

White stockings.

Unblocked satin ballet shoes, scarlet.

Hair : Parted in the centre, plaited into a ' door-knocker ' and
    a wreath of small flowers to tone with the dress worn well
    back on the head.

CLOWN, PANTALOON AND HARLEQUIN
IN A VICTORIAN PANTOMIME
(*From ' Punch ', 1859*)

George :

    Buff or grey peg-top trousers.

    Blue or black coat.

    Frilled shirt.

    Stock.

    Top-hat.

Hair parted at the side and brushed up in front.
Mutton-chop whiskers.

Clown and Pantaloon :

Footmen's dress with knee-breeches and frogged coats.
Clown and Pantaloon wigs and make-up.

Pierrot :

White Pierrot dress with white ruff and black skull-cap.
White stockings and white unblocked ballet shoes.
White make-up.

Harlequin :

Spangle Harlequin dress.
Black ruff.
Black skull-cap.
Belt and pouch.
Black satin cloak.

LES ANGÉLUS DU PRINTEMPS

(Music by Paul de Maleingreau.)

LES ANGÉLUS DU PRINTEMPS

It is the month of May, when strange things are stirring and strange feelings waken in most unexpected bosoms.

The Scene is the square of a small town in Southern France. A flight of steps leads into a church up left. At the centre back is the door of a house, above it a curtained window.

It is the dawn of May Day, when the children and young girls bring flowers and lighted candles in a procession to the church in the village square. It is also the dawn of market day, when the vegetable and flower stalls are bright with country produce, and the little ladies and gentlemen of the town go a-marketing.

The characters are :

THE WANDERING IMMORTALS

Pierrot	..	..	..	.. ⎱ *The Spirits of Love*
Columbine	..	..	..	.. ⎰ *and Beauty*
Scaramouche		..	..	.. *The Spirit of Comedy*

MORTALS

The Beadle
The Market Woman
A Country Maidservant
A Young Peasant
Country Men and Women
Townspeople, Ladies and Gentlemen
Children
Nursemaids

SCENE I

A.

L'Angélus du Matin

The village square is wrapt almost in darkness.

As the curtain rises, Pierrot, Columbine and Scaramouche are discovered as shadowy figures, asleep, leaning against each other, down left. They wandered into the town the night

before, and, being unable to find a lodging, slept in the square.
At the back a bulky form leans against a wall, also asleep.
It is the Beadle.

A faint sound of the Angelus bell is heard, and the first dim
light of the dawn grows. The Beadle wakes with a start, and
jangles his bell, a little peevishly ; these dawns are cold, even
in May.

The light grows a little more, and Pierrot and Columbine
wake gradually. They yawn and stretch, stand up and greet
each other rather sleepily. Scaramouche wakes with a grunt ;
he is none too good-tempered in the early morning.

The Beadle rings his bell more noisily.

From up left and down right the country people begin to
arrive with their produce of flowers and fruit. The Market
Woman is with them. They are tired and sleepy with their
walk in the darkness from the fields where they gathered their
wares. But as the light grows they become more animated.
The Young Peasant and the Maidservant are with them. She
goes into a house door, at centre back, and blows a kiss to
him as she disappears.

Some one points to where the sky is brightening each
moment ; they must get on with their work, to be ready in
the market at sunrise.

Suddenly, they see the Immortals in their midst. These
disreputable players again ! The Beadle rings his bell furiously, bidding them begone. They plead to be allowed to
stay in the town for May Day. Columbine says that she
has brought her flowers for the May Day procession, but the
Beadle is adamant.

Reluctantly, and a little sadly, the players wander away
and out of sight up left. But something tells us that we shall
see them again. It takes more than a Beadle to discourage
the Immortals.

Now there is a bustle among the country people. Some go
off up right, and return with a wooden table ; others bring
poles and a brightly-coloured awning. In a moment the
flower and vegetable stall is set up, in another it is bright with
country flowers and fruit, and the Market Woman is seated
beside it under her striped umbrella, her knitting in her hand.

Again some one points to the sky. The sunrise at last. May Day is dawning. The men stand bare-headed as the sun rises in its full glory and floods the little square with light. Gaiety is everywhere at last ; the world is awake.

Sounds of a procession are heard approaching, and a band of children and young girls in white dresses appears, each carrying a bunch of spring flowers and a lighted candle. It is the May Day procession of the children, headed by a boy carrying a pole decked with greenery, flowers, and ribbons. The procession passes up the steps into the church. The little town is ready for the work and play of the day.

The morning Angelus is passed.

(The curtains close for a moment to denote the passing of the hours.)

B.   SCENE II

MATINÉE (PROMENADE)
Folâtreries dans la Rosée

It is the middle of the morning. The ladies of the town arrive to do their shopping in the market-place. They are prim little figures, carrying baskets and reticules. With them are those dear old gentlemen and crusty colonels who inhabit quiet country towns.

They approach the Market Woman, inquire the price of flowers and vegetables this morning. A little pleasant bargaining is taking place, when a queer sound of piping is heard. The bargaining stops abruptly.

The piping continues, and we see that it is Pierrot. He has a shepherd's pipe, and is playing a wicked jaunty tune. Dancing to himself and calling the prim little townspeople away from their neat little lives to some memory of dancing on dewy lawns on May Days long ago.

Their feet begin absurdly halting dance steps, and each picks up some flowers or a vegetable from the stall and, with it, begins a rather formal and prim little dance. Their joints are stiff ; they are unaccustomed to dancing in any form, let

5

alone a Maytime dance with flowers and fruit, but the piping
goes on, and in spite of themselves they continue to dance
until they are in a circle. The Beadle and the Market Woman,
rather ponderously, join in.

Into the middle of the circle flits a white figure, like a
flying dove : it is Columbine poised airily. Now Pierrot is
beside her. And he tells her the old, old story of the spring,
the one that begins ' I love you.'

Something thrills the prim little ladies ; they step coyly
out of the circle and stand waiting in something of a flutter.

The little old gentlemen and the colonels follow them with
jaunty steps, and, falling upon their knees, repeat the old, old
story, ' I love you.'

Columbine and Pierrot flit among the couples, spreading
magic wherever they go. Then suddenly they disappear, off
up left, behind the church.

The ladies and gentlemen tread a sprightly dance together,
which somehow leads them to surround the Beadle and the
Market Woman, and he, kneeling a trifle painfully beside her,
declares more sonorously than them all, ' I love you.'

Suddenly the piping ceases. The little ladies, the old
gentlemen and the colonels, the Beadle and the Market
Woman are dumbfounded. How came they into these un-
seemly situations ? Surreptitiously each one places the
flowers or fruit into his or her shopping-bag. The Market
Woman returns to her seat, the Beadle to his place beside the
church steps. Every one hopes that no one noticed his or her
inexplicable lapse from decorum. There must be something
odd in the air of the first of May.

Primly and self-consciously they disappear off right to
finish the day's shopping in a less dangerous locality.

The Beadle goes on his round, the Market Woman knits a
trifle feverishly.

Columbine and Pierrot steal on together, hand in hand,
delighted at the success of their prank upon the town that
tried to turn away the Immortals.

Then they, too, disappear.

(And again for a moment the curtains close.)

SCARAMOUCHE
IN 'LES ANGÉLUS DU PRINTEMPS'

C.

Scene III

L'Angélus de Midi

(L'Ardente Sérénade)

The square is golden with midday sun, and empty. The sound of a guitar is heard, and there enters, from up right, Scaramouche, playing a serenade, swaggering, gallant, and distinctly disreputable.

He circles the stage and then places himself beneath the window. His song grows more alluring, and, surely enough, the curtains part, and there looks out the rosy face of the comely Country Maidservant. Scaramouche ceases his song, speaks to her, and begs her to come down to him, telling her how pretty she is.

But now there enters, angrily, the Young Peasant. What is this vulgar player doing making love to his little sweetheart ? He will box his ears for him ! They are about to set upon each other when the midday Angelus sounds. They cease ; the peasant boy pulls off his cap and stands with bowed head. Scaramouche waits a moment, and then makes a tactful and unostentatious exit up right. He simply is not there when the peasant looks up again to continue the fight which the Angelus interrupted.

The hidden girl looks out once more. She sees below her own sweetheart, not the strange swaggering gallant who was making love to her a moment before. She disappears, and then trips out of the door of the house to him. In a moment they are gone together.

Once more Scaramouche's haunting tune is heard, and back he comes, smiling to himself, swaggering still, and wanders on out of sight up left. There are other windows, and France is full of pretty little maids, ready to hear his serenades in the lazy noontide sunlight.

(The curtains close.)

D.

Scene IV

Berceuse d'Après-midi

It is afternoon, the time of siesta ; sleep is beginning to
steal over the quiet town. There enter four neat little nursemaids, carrying four neat little babies from up left. They
walk sedately and carefully, and rock their charges, until they
whisper, ' Hush ! He is asleep.'

The children, too, are tired of their May Day games. They
enter, also from left, sleepily humming a nursery rhyme, and
seat themselves on the ground, leaning against each other.
' You and I must go to sleep,' they sing. ' This eye and that
is closing.' ' You and I are going to sleep.' And they rock
themselves a moment and are asleep.

Pierrot and Columbine wander on, also humming a little
sleepy song. They kiss like two children, slide to the ground
back to back, rocking to and fro against each other. The
Market Woman nods. The children nod, the nursemaids nod
as they rock the sleeping babies. And, at the back, the
Beadle nods majestically—until, as the rocking-tune dies
away, sleep gathers them all.

(The curtains close.)

E.

Scene V

L'Angélus du Soir

(Prélude—Hymne—Crépuscule)

The sun has left the square. Evening has come. The
Beadle enters from up left to centre. The peasants return
wearily from their work, or May Day celebrations, and slowly
mount the steps into the church, passing across the stage from
up right. They are heavy-footed in the evening. The Beadle
takes up his position beside the church steps. The little ladies
pass also towards the church, whence the ghost of a hymn
comes out. More peasants follow, and the old gentlemen also

go into the church for the evening service ; and, lastly, the Beadle mounts the steps and disappears. When all are there we hear the organ playing. The Market Woman is left listening, crossing herself as she hears the sound of the service coming from within the church.

The music swells and the sound of the hymn pours out into the evening air. At its climax the children come out in procession. The May Day service and celebrations are over. The townspeople and peasants, too, pour out of the church, and as the sunset light gilds the square, it is full of people, a gay and happy scene.

For a moment a queer little tune is heard once more, and suddenly at the top of the steps, lit by the light of the sinking sun, stand the three Immortals, looking down on the quiet town they have visited for a brief day.

But dusk is falling. Mysterious shadows begin to wrap the square. The bright colours fade and the human people slip away into the gathering darkness. Homes call when evening comes. No one is left in the square.

No one ? Yes, the three wandering Immortals are there, still forgotten of men, and in the gloaming some strange radiance seems shed about them : the radiance of the old magic, perhaps. They leave the church steps and come to the centre of the square.

A horn sounds faintly in the distance. Pierrot recognizes the call. He bids his fellow-travellers pass on with him. There are other towns to visit with the Spirits of Love and Laughter. It may be a long road. But it is a gay road. It seems as if some vision leads them as they pass out. And the Angelus becomes a carillon of far and faery bells, ringing down the ages, calling into the Future : the Angelus of the Eternal Spring.

(The curtains close for the last time.)

NOTES ON MUSIC

Music Required :

 Les Angélus du Printemps ..   ..   Paul de Maleingreau

  (Published by J. & W. Chester, Ltd.)

A. *L'Angélus du Matin.*

The Immortals sleep	4 bars
The Beadle's bell	3 bars
Columbine and Pierrot wake, then Scaramouche ..	12 bars
The Beadle's bell	2 bars
Entrance of peasants..	11 bars
The Beadle tells Immortals to be gone	4 bars
They plead to stay	4 bars
They exeunt, followed by Beadle	8 bars
Two peasants exeunt to fetch stall	2 bars
Do. do.	2 bars
Do. do.	4 bars
Re-enter with table	2 bars
Re-enter with poles	3 bars
Re-enter with canopy. Arrange stall, bring vege-	
tables, etc. Market Woman settles herself ..	8 bars
All in position waiting sunrise	5 bars
The procession	16 bars

B. *Matinée.*

Entrance of ladies to stall	5 bars
Entrance of gentlemen	3 bars
Conversation and bargaining	4 bars
Entrance of Beadle	2 bars
All collect purchases	2 bars
Pierrot plays his pipe and appears down left ;	
crosses down right. Ladies and gentlemen	
feel something queer is happening	12 bars
Ladies and gentlemen dance and form a circle ..	12 bars
Columbine runs in to centre from up left	3 bars
Pierrot's declaration of love	4 bars
Ladies look at gentlemen, who kneel	8 bars
Gentlemen's declaration	5 bars
Pierrot and Columbine run among them and exeunt	6 bars

Ladies and gentlemen dance in couples .. .. 12 bars
Beadle and Market Woman down to centre .. 4 bars
Beadle's declaration of love .. .. 5 bars
They all recover themselves and exeunt .. .. 12 bars
Pierrot and Columbine return and exeunt again 5 bars

C. *L'Angélus de Midi.*

Scaramouche enters and goes down left, playing.. 10 bars
He turns up centre .. .. 4 bars
He calls up to the window .. .. 4 bars
The girl looks out .. .. 4 bars
He says : ' You come down. You are pretty ' .. 8 bars
The Peasant Boy enters and threatens Scaramouche 8 bars
Midday bell. Scaramouche and boy still. Then
    exit Scaramouche .. .. 7 bars
The boy turns. The girl looks out. Comes down.
    Exeunt .. .. 5 bars
Re-entrance and exit of Scaramouche .. .. 14 bars

D. *Berceuse d'Après-midi.*

Entrance of nursemaids, rocking babies .. .. 11 bars
Entrance of children and sit .. .. .. 8 bars
' You and I go to sleep, this eye that eye closes.
    You and I go to sleep.' Rock .. .. .. 14 bars
Pierrot and Columbine enter, kiss, sit and rock .. 6 bars
Market Woman sleeps, and they all rock .. .. 5 bars

E. *L'Angélus du Soir.*

Enter Beadle .. .. 5 bars
Enter peasants and into church .. .. .. 8 bars
Beadle moves down .. .. 5 bars
More peasants .. .. 6 bars
Ladies and gentlemen enter and into church .. 3 bars
Beadle up and into Church .. .. 6 bars
The hymn ; Market Woman listens .. .. 6 bars
Children out, followed by crowd .. .. .. 5 bars
Immortals appear on steps .. .. 3 bars
Crowd moves about and gradually disappears .. 6 bars
Immortals to centre .. .. 2 bars
They hear the call. Pierrot points the way. They
    hear the echo and go .. .. 13 bars

PROPERTY PLOT

Stage :

Flight of steps leading into church half up left. Rostrum and
steps leading off.

Off Up Right :

Wooden table, with slots for poles.
4 wooden poles.
Striped awning.
Baskets of vegetables and fruit.
Stool.

Hand :

Bell	..	..	..	..	.. *Beadle*
Knitting	..	..	..	..	.. *Market Woman*
Guitar	..	..	..	..	.. *Scaramouche*
Flowers	..	..	..	..	.. *Columbine*
Flowers	..	..	..	..	.. *Children*
Lighted candles	..	..	..		.. *Ditto*
Shopping baskets	..	..	..		.. *Ladies and Gentlemen*
Shepherd's pipe	..	..	..		.. *Pierrot*
4 Babies	..	..	..	..	.. *Nursemaids*

COSTUME

Pierrot :

White Pierrot suit (trousers and loose coat).
Ruffle.
Skull-cap.
White stockings and shoes.
White make-up.

Columbine :

Tarlatan ballet dress (white), with fitting bodice ; skirt ankle
length.
Tights.
Ballet shoes.
Wreath of roses.

Scaramouche :

Black knee-breeches.
Black jacket fastening down front (buttoned).
Leather sword-belt (with or without sword).

Small white ruffle.

Black circular cloak, knee length.

Soft cap like a tam-o'-shanter, pleated into a band round head.

Black stockings.

Heeled shoes with large rosettes.

White make-up with small moustache and tiny pointed beard on chin.

(Scaramouche is really a masked character, but make-up will probably prove more satisfactory.)

Beadle :

Dark blue knee-breeches.

Red coat, skirted and caped, with large side-pockets.

White waistcoat.

Cocked hat.

White cotton or woollen stockings.

Black buckled shoes.

(See Dickens : *Sketches by Boz*.)

Market Woman :

Full red skirt to ground, dark blue apron.

Fitting bodice.

Small black woollen shawl crossed over chest.

Coloured handkerchief tied under hair behind, or under chin.

White stockings.

Black shoes, heavy and flat-heeled.

Peasant Women :

Full, long, coloured skirts, aprons.

White or coloured blouses.

Cross-over shawls.

Handkerchiefs on head, some with white head handkerchiefs tied under chin, below wide, low-crowned, straw hats. Some lace caps.

White stockings.

Black shoes.

Peasant Men :

Dark blue trousers.

Blue blouse shirts, belted.

Handkerchief at neck.

Soft caps, or rather wide felt hats.

Coloured socks.
Heavy dark shoes.

Nursemaids :

Long coloured print dresses, with fitting bodices.
Large white aprons, with bib, and ends tied behind and hanging
down.
White caps with streamers, or big black bows on the top of the
head, with long streamers.
White stockings.
Black buttoned boots.

Children :

Full white muslin dresses.
Coloured sashes.
Hair ribbons.
White stockings.
Black shoes.

Boy :

Brown knickers.
White shirt.
Stockings and shoes.

Ladies :

Walking costume, 1812-20 (or the 'seventies, if preferred).
Dresses, high-waisted, long, tight sleeves.
Short-waisted jackets, or short capes.
Skirts straight and clinging.
Flowered bonnets, or hats tied under chin.
Sunshades.
Light stockings.
Flat sandal shoes.

Gentlemen :

Buff breeches, tight-fitting to below knee, or close-fitting
trousers, 1812–20.
Tail coats, dull red or brown, double-breasted, with high collar.
Light waistcoats, striped or flowered.
Frilled shirts.
White stockings.
Black pumps.
Top-hats.

THE LADYE OF ARMOR

*(Music selected from Capriol Suite, by Peter Warlock ;
Ballet Suite, by Handel, arranged by Sir Thomas
Beecham.)*

This Play has been performed at the Scala Theatre, London ; Ambassadors Theatre, London ; Memorial Theatre, Stratford-upon-Avon ; and at the Open Air Performances in Hyde Park, under the auspices of The League of Arts.

At the original performance the cast was as follows :

The Lady	*Irene Mawer*
Jamin, her Jester ..	*Ruby Ginner*
The Comte de Villemarqué	*Oonah Todd Naylor*
The Comte de Toussaint	*Marion Gillett*
Geber, the Alchemist ..	*Molly Shannon*

Produced by the author.

THE LADYE OF ARMOR

Scene: A Curtain set of as rich a colour as possible. Two stone seats with bright-coloured cushions stand half-way down left and right. In the opening centre-back is a raised dais, having on it a great carven chair with a small table beside it, and, behind, a sky-cloth, lit a deep blue, as if we saw beyond a window to the far sky of the fabulous land of Armor, which, like Lyonesse, now lies under the sea. All the chivalry, poesy, and romance of those lost lands colour the Western Seas, and the bells of their hidden towers ring eerily. This little play, for all its simplicity, should try to catch and hold some echo of the love, laughter, colour, and high romance that were lost when the seas swept over the hidden land of Armor. All the colour and graciousness of those days of the Courts of Love are to be found in the Italian illuminated pictures and fresco paintings of the fourteenth and fifteenth centuries. The people of those pictures live and move and speak for us in the tales of The Decameron *and the sonnets of the Italian poets. Here the names are French, for Armor was part of the land which we now know as Brittany, but their clothes are painted by Italian artists, and their lives penned by Italian poets. Here we try to catch them for a brief moment upon an English stage.*

The Characters are:

The Ladye of Armor
Jamin, her Jester
The Comte de Villemarqué, wealthy
    but stout
The Comte de Toussaint, gallant but
    foolish
Geber, the Moorish Alchemist, who
    has wisdom

*Suitors
for the
hand of
the Ladye*

A Chamberlain
Ladies and Gentlemen of the Court of Armor
Three Pages of the Suitors

Four Little Pages of the Ladye
A Troup of Jesters

Scene : The Great Hall of the Castle of Armor.

A.   As the curtain rises it seems that we are surely looking
on some picture from an old tapestry or illuminated missal
work. There is no movement at all. The Ladye of Armor
sits in her great chair, alone in the Castle Hall, save that, at
her feet, there crouches Jamin, her Jester. He is as immovable as his mistress, gazing at her as a dog might do. The
Ladye is evidently thinking dreamily—her long, white hands
lying idly on the arms of the chair, her high jewelled head-
dress still against the dark wood of the chair. From beneath
it her pale face shines out almost childlike, for all the regal
carriage of her head. A great lady is so high above the
world that she looks upon it from afar as a child might turn
the pages of a book, wondering sometimes, perhaps, whether
she is really a woman as others are : a woman to love, to
suffer, to laugh, to command, and to surrender. With a
half-sigh the Ladye turns her head slightly to look at Jamin,
the playfellow of her childhood, the strangely dear plaything
of her lonely womanhood. He is looking up at her, all his
devotion in his eyes, and as she looks at him he seems inspired,
seizes the pen and scroll that are ever ready to his hand, and
adds a line to the poem in which he is always celebrating the
beauty of his Ladye. His body may be misshapen, but his
heart is a man's and his soul a poet's.

B.   Then there arrive the four favourite little Pages of the
Ladye—stiff, formal figures in their brocade doublets. The
first carries a silver bowl of water in which she dips her
fingers, the next the silken cloth upon which she wipes them,
the third fresh flowers to lay in her hands, the fourth a
mirror that she may see her beauty needs no fresh adorning.
She looks into the mirror, and smiles to see that she is indeed
beautiful, then shrugs her shoulders a little wearily to think
that she sits alone for all her beauty.

Jamin watches her every movement, and we learn that he

SCENE IN A MEDIEVAL BANQUETING HALL

SUGGESTING COSTUMES FOR ' THE LADYE OF ARMOR '

reads, not only her movements, but her very thoughts, for
he has watched her for so long.

The ceremony of the hand-washing over, the Pages stand
aside, as formal figures, right and left of the dais, and the
Ladye is ready to receive her Court.

C.   The first to enter is one of the Court ladies. She appears
up right, and passes down right, slim and willowy in her
long, clinging dress and 'steeple' head-dress. She moves
up in front of the Ladye and curtsies low. But as she rises
she catches sight of the first gentleman, who now enters up
left, and the naughty little creature slips away down right
waiting for her cavalier to join her. This he does, after
making his bow to the Ladye on the dais. Then, from up
right and left, come more groups of ladies and gentlemen.
All make their obeisances to the Ladye, and then move down
right and left, forming picturesque groups on and about the
two seats down right and left. In movement they have been
very formal and conventional, but we see from their faces that
they are as human and laughter-loving as all those people of
whom Boccaccio told his tales. The Ladye acknowledges their
salutations a trifle wearily—she has played this game so often.

D.   Now there come tumbling on a band of jesters, strange,
motley creatures, who must always be turning head over
heels, capering, or dancing. They run in, from up left to down
right, turning cartwheels and somersaults as they come.
They finish with a few steps of a ridiculous dance, then with
a jump they all face up stage together, run up centre, and
make their bows to the Ladye, with their backs to the
audience. At a sign from Jamin they run down stage left
and right, making odd groups against the proscenium.

E.   For now there arrives with solemn tread a very Malvolio
of a Chamberlain, with his long wand of office. If you want
to know *just* what he is like read Maria's description of
Malvolio. Having entered pompously from up left he
establishes himself half-way down right and solemnly
addresses the Ladye with :

6

'Madonna, but there are three gentlemen desirous to
marry with you.'

The Ladye is intrigued. The Chamberlain always makes
her laugh, anyway, and here is a diversion, if nothing more.
So she replies at once :

'Three gentlemen to marry me ?　By all means show
them in.'

The Chamberlain crosses pompously to beside the entrance
up left, and waves a dignified hand to signify that the
gentlemen are welcome to enter. The ladies and gentlemen
of the Court settle themselves expectantly to watch. Suitors
are frequently so *very* entertaining. The pages are waved
away out of sight.

F.　Monsieur le Comte de Villemarqué heads the procession
of suitors. He is short of stature, red of countenance,
pompous, and—in a whisper the ladies say it—fat ; but
obviously very wealthy. He is followed by a page carrying
a silver casket. Next, serious, self-contained and handsome,
comes the tall, dark figure of the Moorish alchemist, Geber.
Even the frivolous little ladies dare not titter at him. He is
followed by an Eastern page, bearing a great heavy carved
wooden box. Finally there arrives—there is no other word
for it—Monsieur le Comte de Toussaint. How exquisite are
his small fair beard and the white bejewelled hand with
which he caresses it from time to time ! How ravishing the
silken perfection of his legs in their pale-coloured tights !
He is not perhaps dignified, but with what an air he disguises
his lack of inches, what languishing glances he throws, rather
indiscriminately perhaps for a suitor, among the Court ladies !
His lute hangs by coloured ribbons from his shoulder. He
is followed by an exquisitely appointed page, carrying a
gilded cage containing a pair of love-birds. The suitors,
entering from up left, pass down left, where they stand
imposingly in a diagonal line, each with his page behind him.

G.　The Ladye sweeps from her chair, all graciousness and
dignity. She curtsies to each of the suitors in turn and prays
them to pass on into the hall that their gifts may be seen

and their suits acknowledged. They pass before her and circle the stage, an imposing procession, each followed by his page. But as they pass her and retire up stage, the Ladye comes down centre, and for a brief moment, showing the sense of humour that lightens the dignity of her days, she says :

' *I* marry one of these ? I hardly think so ! '

But, nevertheless, she sweeps back to her chair on the dais, and motions to the Chamberlain that she is prepared to consider the gifts, and the gentlemen.

Jamin has been watching, watching all the time ; like some faithful dog he senses danger for his mistress among all these fine gentlemen. She is so young, so impressionable, but not even he knows how wise or how foolish.

H (*1*). The Chamberlain motions to the page of the Comte de Villemarqué to approach. The Comte himself, standing somewhat self-consciously up left, bridles a little, knowing that for wealth no other gift can approach his. Roughly speaking, the others have no chance. The two remaining suitors, now standing up right with their pages, seem strangely unimpressed, however. But the ladies, gentlemen, and jesters are all agog with excitement to see what the fat old man has to offer.

The page walks to the centre of the stage and holds up the silver casket for every one to see. Then he approaches the Ladye, bows deeply, and lays the casket into her hands and retires beside his master.

H (2). The Ladye, pleased as a child with a toy with the rarity of the casket, opens it and gives a gasp of delight at the wonder and richness of what lies within. She draws out a necklace of rubies and pearls—it is indeed marvellous and surely almost priceless. She raises it, and, laying it against her dress, passes down from the dais and round the right of the stage, showing the ladies the wonder of the jewels. They are suitably impressed. ' Marvellously rare and exquisite,' they say.

The Ladye pauses down right, and, holding up the jewels,

she laughs her delight to Jamin, still watching on the steps of the dais. He bows to her. ' Ah, yes, Madonna, the jewels are magnificent ; but here waits the gentleman.'

The Ladye turns away, sighing. She had omitted to remember the gentleman !

Now the Comte advances ponderously, glowing with pleasure at the expected success of his gift, and possibly also from unwonted emotion and exertion. When he reaches a suitable spot well in the centre of the hall, and beside the Ladye, he slowly and carefully lowers himself on to one knee. It is usual to make a proposal of marriage in this position, but he does not find it easy to attain ! However, there he is at last, and comparatively comfortable.

The Ladye has become engrossed once more in the splendour of workmanship and the glorious colour of the jewels. She turns with a start to find their donor on his knees beside her. She composes herself to listen to his wooing. It is not very original.

' I love you,' he begins. A good firm and deliberate phrase that. You can't get it wrong. Then he continues :

' If you will marry me, I will give you jewels like those in piles, like this——'

Once more he has turned her attention from himself to the jewels, which in some strange way seem to fascinate her. In her wonder at their richness she seems half-oblivious of the not very heroic nobleman kneeling beside her.

I. Jamin feels a danger for his beloved mistress. Suppose in her wonder at the jewels she overlooks the fact that the man beside her is nothing more than a gross moneybag. He must save her, bring her back to herself before she commits some folly which she will ever regret.

His eye falls upon the flowers the page brought, where they lie upon a table near her chair : lilies, her favourite flower. He seizes one, and standing half behind her, out of sight himself, he slips it into her free hand. She starts as if waking from a dream. Then she holds up before her, in one hand, the glittering jewels, in the other the slim white beauty of the flower. She compares them for a moment, and then the

A MEDIEVAL COURT FOOL
COSTUME FOR JAMIN IN 'THE LADYE OF ARMOR.'

jewels slip unheeded into the outstretched hands of the astonished Comte, and the lily is laid against her cheek.

As she sweeps back to her chair, she looks a moment at Jamin and understands his message and his gift, and smiles to reassure him. She will always choose beauty before wealth. Jamin sighs with relief for one danger averted. The enraged and almost apoplectic Comte de Villemarqué regains his feet with considerable difficulty, and then stalks, raging, from the hall, where his wealth has been held as of little worth beside a paltry flower. His page follows him, and a whisper of amusement passes round the Court. Jamin is back at his Ladye's feet as she sits once more in her great chair.

J.   Now the jesters, unable to keep still any longer, bounce out from their positions against the proscenium, right and left, and, running up to the foot of the dais, look up laughing at the Ladye.

'Did she like him?' 'Wasn't he odd?'

They chatter, but Jamin motions them to be quiet for the other suitors are waiting, and they sit down, cross-legged, at the foot of the dais.

The Chamberlain motions the black page of the Alchemist to bring forward his master's gift.

The page, advances, bows to the Ladye and lays his great oak box down in the middle of the stage. He bows and retires. The box has a mysterious and fascinating appearance. It might contain anything. The ladies cannot resist the temptation. They cluster round it like a flock of bright-coloured, inquisitive birds. They touch it and whisper together : 'What is it? More jewels, even rarer than the Count's? Priceless embroideries from the East?' Now the jesters have crawled up and, poking inquisitive heads and fingers between the kneeling figures of the ladies, they speculate about the mysterious box.

But now Jamin advances and waves them all away. It is a gift to his Ladye. No one shall touch it. He stands with one foot on the lid, and then bows to the Ladye to approach.

K.   She sails down once more from her chair. But as she
kneels beside the box, her laughing, exquisite face looks more
than ever like a child's. She seems to say laughing :
  ' My box, I think ! '
  But at last she opens it, and all the ladies, gentlemen, and
jesters crowd round to see. Jamin watches anxiously. What
has the Eastern brought to tempt his mistress ? What must
he fight this time ?
  The Ladye looks in the box, and draws back a moment in
sheer delight. They all peer over her shoulder anxiously,
as, triumphantly, she lifts up—not jewels, nor silks, but—a
great book ! The ladies are bored. The gentlemen smile.
The jesters give it up altogether. A book as a gift from a
wealthy suitor to the Ladye of Armor ! They turn away.
The ladies and gentlemen make a group down right by the
proscenium, with backs to the audience, and another up left,
again talking together without showing their faces. The
jesters climb on to the backs of the seats and wait develop-
ments. Geber stands motionless in the background.
  Jamin, as always, watches his mistress. She rises, en-
thralled with wonder of the book. She carries it away down
left and, slipping almost to the ground, rests the heavy
illuminated book upon her knee, as she pores delightedly
over the wisdom and science and astrology hidden in its
pages.

L.   Now Geber approaches her. For a moment Jamin loses
his head. The dog of an infidel shall not so much as approach
his mistress ; and he meets him centre, with a threatening
gesture of denial. But the tall, dark man hardly notices
the interference of a mere servant. He looks down on him
a moment and then passes on, almost over him, to the Ladye.
  She rises and, still engrossed in the illuminated pages of
the book, curtsies absent-mindedly to the Moor. He makes
her a serious obeisance and, bowing, says :
  ' The book and all his wisdom are hers if she will but give
herself to him in return.'
  She scarcely notices him, but turns away to scan the pages
once more. Wisdom and learning spread before the eyes of

a lonely woman are unexplored channels, fascinating and alluring.

M. Jamin sees her danger again, and, despairing of what to do to save her, his hand touches the scroll of his poem. In a flash of inspiration he adds one more line and, passing round behind her, slips the scroll into her hand, the book she holds resting upon her other arm. The sight of the scroll brings her back to earth. She slips the book back almost heedlessly into the hands of its owner, unrolls the script and reads the poem. As she reads, tears seem to gather in her eyes, although she smiles. Poetry touches her heart ; wisdom had only stirred her intellect.

Geber bows himself gravely away, followed by his page.

As the Ladye crosses the stage preparing to return to her great chair, Jamin follows her. Will she give him one look to say that she understands the poet as well as the poetry ?

She turns. She looks at him indeed, but it is no child whom he faces now. It is a woman who understands his love—all of it. But a woman set apart in a great carven chair in a great hall of a great land, while he must sit for ever at her feet. As she passes by him once more he falls on his knees before that look and, raising a corner of her sweeping robe, kisses it very reverently.

N. Once more the Ladye is back, smiling, on the dais. Two of her gentlewomen run to her, questioning her about the great, grave Alchemist. But she shakes her head and will not answer them. The gentlemen move to stand on either side of the dais. This last little fellow should prove amusing to watch.

For now the Chamberlain has called upon the page of the third suitor to produce his master's gift. The Comte de Toussaint tunes his lute and places himself up left, ready to approach the Ladye with music when she shall have taken in the rare subtlety of his gift.

The page places the gilded cage of love-birds well in view, down right, and for a moment the jesters and the ladies gather round the cage ecstatically. ' The exquisite things ! '

they exclaim to each other. 'Love-birds! The perfect
suitor's gift—emblem of true love.' They do not seem to
notice that the poor birds must sing in a gilded cage and can
never fly into the sunlight.

O.　　But attention wanders from the birds to their donor. With
an elegant swagger, and accompanied by his own playing upon
his lute, Monsieur le Comte de Toussaint encircles the stage
and approaches the Ladye of Armor. At the foot of the dais,
right, he swings his lute away behind his back and flings
himself into an attitude upon one knee. The ladies titter.
The men can hardly forbear to strike the little coxcomb.
Then, having finally caressed his little fair beard to an elegant
point, he speaks in floweriest gesture.

'I love you, Madonna,' he announces, barely looking at
the object of his love. 'My heart is at your most exquisite
feet.'

The Ladye's laughter has rapidly been getting the better
of her. And as his most flowing gesture indicates her feet,
she picks up her dress and runs away on them, leaving the
discomfited nobleman wondering whether she understood
him or not. But on discovering that she has merely run
down to the bird-cage, and is playing delightedly with his
gift, he concludes that she has, and follows her down
remarking as he arrives:

'Ah, the trifle of the birds—a mere nothing. But *I* gave
them to you. . . .'

The Ladye remembers his presence, but being now engrossed with the beauty of the birds' plumage, and thinking
of the message of love they bear, she does not notice him
much. They are the emblem of love, that strange thing from
which it seems she is ever to be debarred. She looks at the
love-birds again; it seems as if she were questioning them
for an answer to the riddle of her own heart. Very absent-
mindedly she extends a hand to the Comte de Toussaint, which
he, in a rapture of self-love, kisses ecstatically.

P.　　This time Jamin does not hesitate a moment. He knows
her well enough to guess what will save her instantly from

a marriage with mere gallantry. He runs to her, where she kneels beside the bird-cage, the Comte still holding her free hand to his lips. And into the ear farthest from that complacent gentleman, he whispers the beginning of a joke. She listens. A smile wakens on her lips and in her eyes. He whispers again, and this time her fingers flutter with laughter, and in so doing tickle the nose of the enraptured lover bending over her hand. He raises his head furiously, to find the Ladye now roaring with laughter before his very eyes. She calls the ladies and the jesters round her and tells *them* the story. They, too, go off into peals and shouts of laughter. Their mouths open indelicately wide, tears trickle down their noses. No sooner do they gain control for a moment than they are off in paroxysms again. What was the joke ? We never know ! For the still laughing ladies and gentlemen exeunt up left and right, passing on the joke from mouth to mouth. The Chamberlain catches it, and his solemn face suddenly cracks with mirth, and *he* totters off, slapping his thighs as though saying, ' Good ! Excellent ! Oh, very good indeed ! '

The highly enraged Comte de Toussaint is obliged almost to fight his way among the weakly laughing crowd in order to make what he hopes is a dignified and protesting exit. If anybody happens to notice him, they merely explode once more in his face. He signs to his page to bring the bird-cage, and, with one last protesting gesture of outraged dignity, disappears.

Q.   The jesters burst into a mad little dance of laughter. If you want to know what they looked like you can see a picture of them in the Bodleian manuscript.

The Ladye, still laughing, mounts to her chair. But laughter is very tiring, and suddenly she is weary. Jamin, down left, sees, and with a gesture drives away the jesters, who disappear, still ridiculously dancing.

R.   Now the great hall is empty, save for the Ladye and her jester. He, too, is suddenly tired. He has saved his mistress from marriage for wealth, wisdom, or gallantry, by giving her instead beauty, poetry, and laughter ; but now it is done, the world seems just as empty for them both. He takes off his jester's cap. For one moment he must be a man, not a motley plaything.

The Ladye has sunk back into her chair. He turns a moment and, unnoticed, watches her.

The laughter fades from her face. Its old wistfulness returns. The great hall is so big, and she so alone. She raises her hand to her heart to still its unquiet beating, and as she does so she touches the scroll of poetry that she had slipped into her dress. Jamin holds his breath, immovable, to see her take it out and read it once more, and touch it lightly with her lips. As she does so her face is lit with a radiance of thought. Not only has that queer creature given her beauty, poetry, and laughter, but a deep, true, and steadfast love as well. Although she be the great Ladye raised high in her chair of state, yet she can never be alone, for he has laid about her life the love of the man's heart which lies hid in the misshapen body of her plaything.

Slowly, as if afraid to waken her from a dream, he, approaches her. Very reverently, he kneels once more at her feet, not only loving her as a servant, but now with all the chivalry of true knighthood. She looks down at him a moment. Then she stretches out her hand, and he lifts it to his lips.

NOTES ON MUSIC

Music Required :

    Ballet Suite. ' The Gods Go a-Begging '   ..   ..   Handel

                (Arranged by Sir Thomas Beecham)

                (Published by Cramer & Co., Ltd.)

    Capriol Suite[1]   ..   ..   Peter Warlock

                (Published by J. Curwen & Sons, Ltd.)

A.   *Capriol Suite.* No. 5.

                Jamin and the Ladye

    Overture before curtain   ..   ..   8 bars

[1] The Capriol Suite is written as a piano duet ; but the numbers required have been arranged as a piano solo and may be obtained in manuscript from J. Curwen & Sons, Ltd., to whom application should be made.

Picture	..	..	..	..	..	..	4 bars
She looks about her ; he watches	..	..	..	4 bars
He writes and she looks at him	..	..	..	4 bars
Return to picture	..	..	..	..	..	2 bars

B. *Ballet Suite.* No. 10. 32 bars, repeating first 10 bars
The Pages' Entrances

| For each of the first three pages | .. | .. | .. | 10 bars |
| For the fourth page .. | .. | .. | .. | .. | 12 bars |

C. Continue from previous number 42 bars. Cut to end
Entrances—Court

Enter First Lady ; curtsy and cross down right	..	12 bars
Enter First Gentleman ; bow and join her	..	8 bars
Enter rest of Court, general movement	..	..	22 bars

D. *Ballet Suite.* No. 5. Play 12 bars and cut to end chord to finish
Entrance of Jesters

All enter and bow to audience	..	..	..	4 bars
Up to Ladye and bow	..	..	..	..	4 bars
To groups at proscenium	..	..	..	..	4 bars

E. *Ballet Suite.* No. 1. Play 30 bars and cut to end
Chamberlain enters and announces Suitors

Entrance and walk round stage to up left	..	8 bars
He says : ' Three gentlemen to marry the Ladye '	3 bars
Ladye : ' Three gentlemen to marry me ? Show them in '	..	..	..	..	..	5 bars

F. Continue from previous number : Allegro movement

Entrance of the Comte de Villemarqué and page	4 bars
Entrance of Geber and page	..	..	..	4 bars
Entrance of Toussaint, and picture of all	..	6 bars

G. *Ballet Suite.* No. 6. Play 24 bars and cut to end chord to finish
The Ladye Greets the Suitors

| Ladye down and curtsy to each | .. | .. | .. | 12 bars |
| They pass round to up right. She says : ' I marry them—oh, no ! ' | .. | .. | .. | .. | 12 bars |

H (1).   *Ballet Suite*.   No. 9.

The Jewels

The page brings forward a casket and takes it to the Ladye	11 bars
She opens it and lifts up the jewels	3 bars

H (2).   *Ballet Suite*.   No. 8.   Play 20 bars and cut to end

The Ladye and Comte de Villemarqué

Ladye comes down ; shows jewels	8 bars
Villemarqué crosses to her and kneels	4 bars
He speaks	8 bars

I.   *Capriol Suite*.   No. 5.   Cut 8 bars.   Play to end

The Giving of the Lily

Jamin takes the lily ; gives it to the Ladye ..	4 bars
She drops the jewels. Exit Comte	6 bars
She returns to chair, followed by Jamin ..	4 bars

J.   *Ballet Suite*.   No. 1.   Cut 30 bars.   Play to end

General Movement and Bringing of the Box

Jesters run up to Ladye and sit on floor	6 bars
General movement	6 bars
Chamberlain signs to Geber's page	2 bars
Page brings forward box	3 bars
Ladies to box	3 bars
Gentlemen to box	4 bars
Jesters to box	4 bars
Jamin comes forward and sends them away ..	6 bars

K.   *Ballet Suite*.   No. 6.   Play 24 bars and cut to end chord to finish

The Ladye to the Box and Take out Book

Ladye down, open box, take out book	12 bars
She crosses to down left	12 bars

L.   *Ballet Suite*.   No. 1.   Play 16 bars and cut to end

The Alchemist

Geber forward. Meets Jamin. On to Ladye ..	8 bars
He speaks	8 bars

M.   *Capriol Suite*.   No. 5.   Play to end

The Giving of the Poem

Jamin finishes his poem and gives it to the Ladye	4 bars

She gives back the book. Geber exit   ..   ..   4 bars
Jamin kneels and kisses her robe. She goes back
   to chair   ..   ..   6 bars

N.   *Ballet Suite*. No. 7. As written without repeat
         General Movement and Presentation of Birds

Gentlemen up to Ladye   ..   ..   8 bars
Jesters on to back of seats   ..   ..   ..   8 bars
Page brings forward bird-cage   ..   ..   ..   4 bars
Ladies, gentlemen, and jesters gather round   ..   12 bars
They open into groups   ..   ..   4 bars

O.   *Ballet Suite*. No. 4.
            The Comte de Toussaint

He moves round stage and kneels to Ladye   ..   18 bars
He says : ' I love you ; I am at your feet.'   ..   8 bars
She runs down to cage   ..   ..   8 bars
He follows and kisses her hand   ..   ..   ..   16 bars

P.   *Capriol Suite*. No. 6.
              The Joke

Jamin thinks of Joke ; comes and whispers to
   Ladye   ..   ..   20 bars
She laughs. Toussaint drops her hand   ..   ..   8 bars
The joke passes round the stage. Exit Toussaint
   and Page   ..   ..   16 bars
Every one laughing ; Chamberlain joins in   ..   16 bars
Every one exit, Jesters last, leaving Jamin down
   left, Ladye in chair   ..   ..   16 bars
         Repeat for Jesters' Dance as required

Q.   *Capriol Suite*. No. 5. As written.
              Finale

FURNITURE

Rostrum, 12 by 4 by 2.
3 tread steps.
High-backed oak chair.
Small carved oak stool or table.
Either 2 stone seats *or* 2 carved oak benches with backs.

Carpet for rostrum and steps.
Drapery to throw over the back of the seats.

PROPERTY PLOT

Rostrum and steps set centre back.

On Rostrum :

Big chair.
To right of chair, small table.
Stone seats set diagonally right and left down stage.

Off Stage, Left :

Oak box containing jewelled book ..	*Page of Alchemist*
Casket containing necklace	*Page of Comte de Villemarqué*
Lute	*Comte de Toussaint*
Bird-cage and 2 love-birds ..	*Comte de Toussaint's Page*
Gold Basin ⎫	
Embroidered Towel ⎬	*Ladye's Four Pages*
Hand Mirror ⎭	
Lily	
Scroll and quill	*Jamin*

COSTUME

Period : Fourteenth to Fifteenth Century

The Ladye :

High-waisted dress with jewelled belt, cut to V at front
and back, neck edged with white fur. Skirt touching
the ground in front and cut to a train at the back.
Long tight sleeves. Dress made in peacock and gold
brocade or peacock velvet.
Butterfly hennin or jewelled head-dress, as in illustration.
White stockings.
Flat leather shoes to match dress.

Court Chamberlain :

Blue velvet houppelande, trimmed brown fur at neck, hem
and wrists. Sleeves very full, narrowing to wrists.
Leather girdle.

Yellow tights.
Black leather shoes with long points.
High circular cap.

Comte de Villemarqué :

Short green and gold brocade tunic cut square in the neck
    to show pleated cream shirt. Sleeves very full and
    slashed to show shirt.
Green surcoat with hanging sleeves trimmed with fur.
Green tights.
Green shoes, pointed.
Gold and black chaperon.

Comte de Toussaint :

Flame and orange-quartered tunic, very short, full in the
    skirt and sleeves.
Tights with one leg flame-coloured, the other in orange and
    flame stripes.
Flame-coloured shoes, pointed.
Fair clubbed wig.
Fair beard and moustache.
Hat with fairly high crown and the brim cut high at the
    back and to a point in front.

Alchemist :

Moorish trousers.
Brocaded and jewelled over-robe.
Loose silk coat, three-quarter length.
Sash.
Moorish shoes.
Dark brown make-up.

Court Ladies and Gentlemen :

In Fifteenth-century Italian dress (see illustration).

Four Jesters to the Ladye :

Tights, with one leg red and the other black.
Short tunics quartered in red and black.
Mummers' capes and hoods with two points, half in red and
    half in red and black check.
Red shoes

Jamin, the Jester :

    Fawn tights.

    Yellow and blue tunic, with elbow-length sleeves lined red, showing green and gold under sleeve. Four tasselled points hanging from tunic ; tassels on sleeves.

    Red and blue quartered hood with ears.

    Short knickers showing below tunic.

    Knee-length boots in gilded leather cut up to a point in front.

                  (See illustration.)

Four Pages to the Ladye :

    Green tights.

    Green and gold short tunics. Square-cut necks, with high inside collar. Puffed sleeves to the elbow, then tight to the wrist.

    Jewelled belts.

    Green shoes.

    Fair wigs with clubbed hair and a fringe (optional).

Page to Comte de Toussaint :

    Flame tights and shoes.

    Short orange tunic with flame-coloured full sleeves.

    Jewelled belt.

    Small round cap, worn well back on the head.

Page to Comte de Villemarqué :

    Gold tights and shoes.

    Green and gold tunic.

    Jewelled belt.

    Dark clubbed wig (optional).

    Green cap.

Page to Geber :

    Either fifteenth century as other pages in different colouring or made up as a negro in Eastern dress.

BELLE PENSÉE-OF-THE-GOLDEN-FLOWERS

(Music selected from the works of H. Farjeon.)

The Play has formed part of the dramatic examinations of the Central School of Speech Training and Dramatic Art, for students taking the Diploma of the London University.

Produced by the author.

BELLE PENSÉE-OF-THE-GOLDEN-FLOWERS

The Scene is an open glade in a wood. At the back, between the trees, is a pool, out of which rise reeds and gold iris flowers. The time is medieval, when great lords and ladies went a-hunting and a-hawking, and when bands of minstrels and jongleurs roamed the country, travelling from one great castle to another to give their entertainments of minstrelsie, dance, and miming.

Now it happened that the Lord of the land wherein lay the wood had a great sorrow, for his daughter, Belle Pensée, was blind. Belle Pensée-of-the-Shadowed-Eyes, they called her, and although it was known that whosoever could cure her blindness would be rewarded by the wealth of princes, even by the hand of Belle Pensée herself, and though many had made a trial, yet none had succeeded. Belle Pensée - of - the - Shadowed - Eyes lived her childhood in darkness, and now in darkness grew to womanhood and beauty.

In those days mortal men and women lived nearer to the world of Faerie than we do to-day, for they were simple-hearted, and oftentimes the Other Folk watched over human lives, and gave a hand to their making, too, if so be it some mortal pleased them well and showed himself of a true faith.

So it is that in this play there are mortals and faery folk, lords and peasantry and minstrels, golden lilies by a forest pool, and through it all the Song-that-openeth-the-Eyes.

These people, then, are thus :

Belle Pensée-of-the-Shadowed-Eyes, known in later days as
    Belle Pensée-of-the-Golden-Flowers
My Lord of the Mount-in-the-Wood, her father
Jean the Harper
Fleur de Lys, a spirit of the pool
Eyes-of-a-Cat, a witch
Coviello, a young man from Italy
A Chamberlain
A Troupe of Jongleurs

Lord and Ladies
Peasantry
  and
Faery Folk of the Pool

A.   As the curtain rises, a band of jongleurs enter, with weary
tread, out of temper, as well as out at heel. They appear
from up right, two pass to down right, and two to down left.
One says, ' I am hungry,' the second agrees disconsolately,
the third says, ' He, over there ' (pointing to where Jean the
Harper is approaching), ' he's always dreaming.' They
gather in the centre to discuss their grievances, and then
break open into a diagonal line, from centre to down left,
pointing to Jean as he is seen in the entrance up right.

B.   There he is, dreaming indeed, his harp slung on his back,
his eyes deep with visions, his mind too full of music to
remember the needs of his followers. He looks back, down
the way he has come, and the light of the sun catches his face,
filling it with radiance. He wanders to the pool, and gazes
down a moment into its clear depths, then off between the
trees which surround it. He turns and faces us, and some
new inspiration seems to come to him with the sound of the
wind in the trees, and the rustle of the reeds.

He takes out his pen and scroll, and writing and listening
alternately, he moves forward composing his song.

Two of the Jesters have moved round behind him ; two
remain down left, now they all move forward and surround
him threateningly, demanding that he shall do something
about the urgent question of obtaining food and shelter. As
they grow more emphatic their gestures rise menacingly, until
he is almost hidden by the gesticulations of his unruly band.
But he is master, and with a single movement he quiets them
and they fall back before his command to silence and patience.
He points to the ground under the trees down right, and,
when they are seated there, he gives them his last loaf of
bread and his own flagon of wine. They snatch the food
greedily, but cheerfully ; then Jean hands them also the scroll
of the song upon which he has been working, and bids them

learn their parts, for they must sing it to-night before the great lord in the castle of the Mount-in-the-Wood.

They make a grotesque little group, some seated, some standing, alternately eating and drinking and laboriously learning, and very quickly fall asleep.

C.   Dusk falls, but a strange radiance fills the glade, as, unearthly and thin, a faery call sounds. Jean starts back. A figure flies like a passing shadow from down right and disappears up left. Jean, bewildered, crosses to down left. Another flash, and a second faery form flits from up left and is gone down right. Jean turns towards the pool. Rising slowly from it, her arms full of golden lilies with their swordlike leaves of green, is Fleur de Lys, the Spirit of the Pool, come to help a mortal in his need.

Jean is drawn irresistibly towards her. She holds out the golden flowers towards him, and he takes them. She bids him bind them to his harp and then, fearlessly, to play the song he hears.

He turns from the pool to the centre, and in a moment he is surrounded by faery shapes. Fleur de Lys calls them from the shadows, as she leaves the pool and floats like a moonbeam from tree to tree. They dance about Jean, weaving their strange faery spell, as he stands binding the lilies to his harp ; in another moment, they are gone, Fleur de Lys into her pool again, and he is alone.

D (1).   The faery radiance fades as a group of peasant folk appear excitedly. They break into chattering groups down left and right, as among them appears a Master of the Ceremonies from the Court. The peasants point derisively at the group of sleeping jongleurs, but the Chamberlain bids them be quiet, for the great lords and ladies are coming this way. The peasants are much excited at the prospect, those on the right run eagerly to the entrance up left to watch for the approach of the lords and ladies. Those on the left run to the jongleurs. They wake them, bid them stir themselves, for My Lord of the Mount-in-the-Wood is approaching, and they must be ready with their entertainment.

The jongleurs wake slowly, but on hearing the news of the coming of the gentry, they run to the centre and, two on each side of the bewildered Chamberlain, proceed to practise their acrobatic feats and tricks.

NOBLEMAN IN HUNTING COSTUME
FOR ' BELLE PENSÉE-OF-THE-GOLDEN-FLOWERS '

D (2). Hastily he bids them all be quiet and to prepare the way for the ladies, to fetch skins and cushions for them to sit on. The jongleurs run to the entrance, as some of the peasants fall back into groups left and right, while others exeunt to fetch cushions as he bade them. The Chamberlain stands up centre, and the Jesters move backwards, bowing before the beautiful ladies as they sweep on like gay birds in their coloured flowing dresses, followed by their gentlemen. A gay picture, colourful and gracious. Jean stands apart, down left, unnoticed, but seeing all. The courtiers are grouped up right.

E.   Now at last comes My Lord of the Mount-in-the-Wood, leading by the hand his daughter, Belle Pensée-of-the-Shadowed-Eyes. She is beautiful as a flower, but her blindness seems to shed a sorrow round her, and her beauty is all unawakened. As she passes, the peasants touch their eyes, saying to one another compassionately, ' She is blind. How sad it is to be so beautiful and always in the darkness.' My Lord and Belle Pensée pass to a raised place or seat up right.

Jean sees her, and the appeal of that sightless face, so full of promise unfulfilled, touches his heart. Henceforth he has eyes for nothing else.

F.   But the jongleurs have keen eyes to business. Here are lords and ladies, who are the source of well-filled pockets and much-needed meals. They step forward and entertain the company with one of their queer little dances. The ladies and gentlemen applaud and throw them money.

Belle Pensée sits silent and sad-faced ; she cannot see their antics. And Jean the Harper stands apart still, enrapt in the beauty of that pale face with its shadowed eyes.

G.   The entertainment over, the Chamberlain steps forward to say that there are two people present who desire to try to restore the sight of the Lady Belle Pensée. May they approach ?

Her father assents almost eagerly ; he always hopes and believes that the miracle will one day be wrought that shall open his child's eyes to the light. Belle Pensée assents wearily. There have been so many trials, so many failures, and still she sits in the dark. The Chamberlain beckons the applicants to approach.

H.   The first to enter is Eyes-of-a-Cat, the Witch. She has a spell that is sure of success. The Lady Belle Pensée must stand in a magic circle, alone in the centre of the wood. Belle Pensée walks listlessly forward as she is bidden. The circle is drawn by the witch about her. She makes grotesque moves and passes before the slight figure. The air grows dark and thunderous. My Lord starts up. The peasants and the ladies shrink back in fear ; then as the darkness lifts, they crowd forward to look into Belle Pensée's eyes. But they are as unlit as ever. The Witch is dismissed ignominiously, amid the jeers of the peasants who follow her off up left. Poor little Belle Pensée awaits the other applicant for her wealth or her hand.

I.   Coviello approaches pompously. He says, ' I have a ring. The Lady Belle Pensée has but to put it upon her finger and her sight is restored.' He places the ring on her finger, the ladies gather anxiously to witness the result and—nothing happens. Belle Pensée feels for the ring, takes it off, and hands it to the Chamberlain, who gives it to its discomfited owner, who makes a slightly undignified exit. Belle Pensée is seated once more beside her father, still blind, and after each attempt a little more listless.

J.   Now the faery call is heard and the radiance fills the wood again. Jean takes his harp and begins to play. A trance falls upon the company, save Belle Pensée, who rises and walks steadily and unhesitatingly towards the music as Jean plays on.

    The figure of Fleur de Lys rises once more from the pool, bidding him remember the golden lilies. He ceases to play, but the music goes on. He unbinds the lilies from his harp and lays them in the arms of Belle Pensée. As he does so, the light dawns in her eyes ; she sees.

    Other figures rise from the pool. They circle about Belle Pensée and crown her with more golden flowers. Jean kneels at her feet, wondering at the miracle that his music and his flowers have wrought, and at the beauty in her awakened face. The music dies away, the Faery Folk are gone, but the light in her eyes remains. Jean moves back, and Belle Pensée is left alone in the centre.

K.   The peasants return to find Belle Pensée-of-the-Shadowed-Eyes no longer, but Belle Pensée-of-the-Golden-Flowers, radiant and smiling. Jean still stands aside. The peasants crowd forward to see her.

PEASANT WOMAN
COSTUME FOR 'BELLE PENSÉE-OF-THE-GOLDEN-FLOWERS'

'A miracle! A miracle!' they cry, as they stoop to kiss her robe. Then they retreat once more in awe. The ladies come forward and lead her to her father.

'Who has done this?' he asks. 'Who seeks the reward?'

The Witch hastens forward, saying, ' My ointment.'
Coviello says, ' My ring.'
But Belle Pensée shakes her head.

L.   She moves slowly and unhesitatingly forward to where
Jean stands alone and unnoticed. And before them all she
kisses his forehead and gives him both her hands. Then she
leads him forward. He has wrought the miracle. He alone
may claim the reward.

The Lord of the Mount-in-the-Wood joins the hands of
Belle Pensée-of-the-Golden-Flowers and Jean the Harper. If
he will claim his reward she is his. Jean kneels to the Lady-
of-the-Shadowed-Eyes, and the pages bring a blue cloak for
the shoulders of the betrothed of Belle Pensée-of-the-Golden-
Flowers. The lords and ladies and the peasantry leave them
alone in the glade.

M.   Jean takes his harp and plays his Faery Song to her once
more. As dusk falls, the faery people rise from the pool and
encircle Belle Pensée-of-the-Golden-Flowers and Jean the
Harper, as he draws her to him.

Just before the curtain falls the jongleurs creep past,
jingling well-filled wallets and munching delicious venison
pasties. As they pass they give a silent blessing to their lost
leader, Jean the Harper. A dreamer he was, but his dreaming
has stood them in good stead this time.

Indeed, it seems that blessed insooth was Jean the Harper,
by the light in the eyes of Belle Pensée-of-the-Golden-Flowers.

And that is the end of this Telling.

NOTES ON MUSIC

Music Required :

A Summer Suite	..	..	..	..	H. Farjeon
Pictures from Greece	..	..	..	..	Ditto
The Four Winds	..	..	..	..	Ditto
A Miniature Sonata in B Flat ..	..	..	Ditto

(Published by Augener & Co., Ltd.)

A. *Summer Suite.* No. 2. First 22 bars only
Entrance of Jongleurs

First two jongleurs enter to down right	4 bars
Second two jongleurs enter to down left	4 bars
They speak, meet centre, open to diagonal line pointing to Jean approaching	14 bars

B. *Summer Suite.* No. 1. Play whole without repeats
Jean the Harper and Jongleurs

Jean enters, looks off, into pool, takes out scroll ..	21 bars
He walks down centre, writing and listening ..	21 bars
Jongleurs move threateningly towards him ..	20 bars
He quiets them with a gesture	2 bars
Points to where they are to sit	3 bars
They sit. He gives them food and the scroll ..	17 bars

C. *Summer Suite.* No. 5. First 39 bars only, with repeat as marked
The Faery Song and Appearance of Fleur de Lys

The faery call	2 bars
Jean starts	2 bars
First faery figure	2 bars
Jean moves left	2 bars
Second faery figure	2 bars
Jean turns to pool	2 bars
Fleur de Lys rises from the pool	4 bars
Jean moves towards her .. ..⎫ She gives him the lilies .. ..⎭	7 bars
She says : ' Play '	1 bar
He turns from pool to centre	3 bars
Fleur de Lys leaves the pool, calling to other faery figures to join her. They all appear	8 bars
They circle round Jean as he binds the lilies to his harp	4 bars
They disappear. Jean moves down left	4 bars

D (1). *Sonata.* 1st Part. Play to Bar 27 without repeat. Cut to Bar 56. Play to end of movement, i.e. 35 bars
Entrance of Peasants

Entrance of peasants	7 bars

Chamberlain speaks	..	..	..	..	..	8 bars
Crowd moves ..	..	..	..	..	..	12 bars
Jongleurs wake ; run centre ; practise tricks				..		7 bars
Chamberlain speaks, sending all to places					..	8 bars
General moves into positions for entrance of lords and ladies			..	..	..	..	..	20 bars

D (2). *Sonata—Minuetto.* 26 Bars without repeats
> *Entrance of Lords and Ladies. General Movement*
> Arrange according to number of performers

E. *Pictures from Greece.* No. 2. Bars 16–29
> *Entrance of My Lord of the Mount-in-the-Wood and Belle Pensée*

F. *Last Part of Sonata.* Bar 34 to end.
> *The Jongleurs Dance*
> Arrange as required.

G. *First Part of Sonata.* Bar 56 to end
> *Jongleurs to places after Dance*
> *Chamberlain announces Eyes-of-a-Cat and Coviello.*

Jongleurs to Places	..	..	..	..	..	7 bars
Chamberlain's announcement		..	..	..	8 bars
General excitement. Chamberlain calls Eyes-of-a-Cat and Coviello			..	..	..	..	20 bars

H. *North Wind from ' The Winds '.* Last 32 bars
> *Eyes-of-a-Cat*

She enters. Says she can open Belle Pensée's eyes				10 bars
Calls her centre	..	..	..	..	..	2 bars
Belle Pensée moves centre	..	..	..	..	2 bars
Witch circles round her, etc.	..	..	..	..	8 bars
Peasants forward to look	..	..	..	..	4 bars
They chase off witch and exeunt after her			..	6 bars

I. *Sonata—Andante—repeat last 12 bars.*
> *Coviello*

| He comes forward | .. | .. | .. | .. | .. | 4 bars |
| Says he has a ring to open Belle Pensée's eyes | | .. | 8 bars |

He puts on ring, but nothing happens	..	..	12 bars
She takes off ring. Chamberlain returns it. Coviello exits. Belle Pensée back to up right. (Repeat of above) ..	..	..	..	..	..	12 bars

J. *Summer Suite.* No. 5. First 27 bars and last 19 bars, without repeats

Jean gives the Flowers to Belle Pensée. The Miracle

The Faery call	..	..	..	..	..	2 bars
Jean remembers	..	..	..	..	..	2 bars
Fleur de Lys rises from pool	..	..	..	2 bars
He takes his harp	..	..	..	..	..	6 bars
He plays	..	..	..	..	..	..	4 bars
He ceases to play, Belle Pensée moves forward	..	4 bars
He lays the flowers in her arms. Her eyes open. He kneels	..	..	..	..	..	7 bars
Fleur de Lys crowns Belle Pensée. She turns to him. He kneels, worshipping her	..	..	8 bars
The faery people surround them and disappear again. Belle Pensée left alone centre	..	11 bars

K. *Pictures from Greece.* No. 2. Bar 30 to end

The Peasants return, rejoicing

Peasants crowd forward and kneel before Belle Pensée	..	..	..	..	..	8 bars
The ladies come forward and lead her to her father	8 bars

L. *Pictures from Greece.* No. 3. Without repeat

Belle Pensée acknowledges Jean. Exit Crowd

Belle Pensée crosses to Jean. Kisses his forehead. Gives him her hands	..	..	..	..	8 bars
She leads him centre. Her father joins their hands. Cloak is brought. Exeunt all ..	..	..	20 bars

M. *Summer Suite.* No. 5. First 4 and last 15 bars

Finale

Summer Suite, No. 5, for Overture, if required.

PROPERTY PLOT

Stage :

Curtain or woodland set.
Opening centre back showing lit sky cloth, or cut tree cloth.
Stone surround for pool, with reeds rising from it.
Bank or seat up right.

Hand :

Sheaf of yellow irises	*Fleur de Lys.*
Crown of yellow irises	*Fleur de Lys, in pool*
Minstrel's harp	*Jean.*
Scroll	*Ditto*
Pen	*Ditto*
Wallet containing bread and flagon of wine	*Ditto*
Ring	*Coviello.*
Skins and cushions for peasants	*Off up left.*
Purses of money	*Lords and Ladies.*
Pies	*Jongleurs, off left.*

COSTUME

Fifteenth Century

Belle Pensée :

Gold brocade dress, high-waisted, cut V front and back, or
tunic-shaped. Long tight under-sleeves, full open over-
sleeves, lined rose.
Flat shoes, rose or gold.
Hair : Short and full, or plaits bound round head.

Jean :

Tights—one red, one green.
Flat shoes—one red, one green.
Red and green quartered tunic with hood. Long tight
under-sleeves ; hanging over-sleeves.
Belt.

Jongleurs :

    Two all in green.
    Two all in red.
    Tights, short tunics, with hoods and belts.

My Lord of the Mount-in-the-Wood :

    Blue, or blue and gold tights.
    Blue and gold brocade tunic, with long sleeves.
    Purple and black surcoat with hanging sleeves trimmed with fur.

Coviello :

    See Comte de Toussaint in ' The Ladye of Armor ', changing colour if required.

Fleur de Lys and Faery People :

    Green draperies.
    Flowers or leaves in hair.
    Bare feet.

Eyes-of-a-Cat :

    Scarlet dress.
    Black cloak with hood.

Ladies :

    Long, high-waisted, or tunic, gowns.
    Tight-fitting sleeves.
    Turban, hood, or steeple head-dresses.
    Various colours, all to tone. Avoid gold or bright green.
      (See illustration for ' The Ladye of Armor.')

Gentlemen :

    Tights.
    Hunting-boots.
    Short brocade tunics. Tight sleeves with open over-sleeve.
    Hawking gloves.
    Round caps with fairly high crowns ; or hats with brim turned up at back and down in front.
    Clubbed hair or wigs.
    Colours mainly rust, brown and green.
               (See illustration.)

Peasants :

> Men : Tights, jerkins (leather or rough material).
> Various coloured hoods.
> Heavy or pointed leather shoes.

> Women : Long full dresses of rough material in clear blues, reds, and greens, caught up into leather girdles, showing underdress.
> Hoods or white handkerchiefs wound round head and neck, with wide-brimmed peasant hat.
> Aprons.
> Bare feet, or heavy shoes and cotton stockings.

> (See illustration.)

THE RED ROSES OF THE REVOLUTION

(Music selected from the works of Chopin.)

The play has formed part of the Examinations for the Diploma in Dramatic Art of the University of London, for students of the Central School of Speech Training and Dramatic Art ; by whom it has been performed in Hyde Park, under the auspices of the League of Arts. It has also formed part of the Dramatic Examinations of the Ginner-Mawer School of Dance and Drama.

In each case the play was produced by the author.

THE RED ROSES OF THE REVOLUTION

Scene: The gardens of a French château. There are gates, up left, forming the entrance to the gardens; and, up right, a broad flight of steps leading to a terrace before the door of the château, or directly into the house itself. We are in the days of the Revolution, but this quiet corner of the world seems untouched by anything save mellow sunlight, and the serenity of lives lived securely in the old régime. Moreover, it is the wedding-day of the young Marquis, and so all thought of the menace of the Revolution has been put far away from the minds of nobles and peasantry alike. How should that half-understood, grim spectre touch the old Lady Marquise, her handsome young son, or the peasantry, who, all their lives, have looked upon the grand old lady as their benefactress, almost as their patron saint? But the thunder-cloud of revolution is rolling over the land, leaving nothing untouched in its passage. Even on this day of sunlight and rejoicing it threatens the security of this quiet corner where, for centuries, the château has stood among its trees.

The persons in the play are:

> The Marquis
> His Bride
> Madame La Marquise, his Mother
> Margot, a peasant girl
> The Leader of the Revolutionaries
> First Lady
> First Gentleman
> Four Peasant Girls
> Other Ladies and Gentlemen, Wedding Guests
> A Band of Revolutionaries, Men and Women

Period—Late Eighteenth Century

A.   As the curtain rises a peasant girl in gala dress, and carrying a basket of red rose petals, runs in, from up left, to the centre. There she stands a moment, tiptoe with excitement. The wedding has taken place, the handsome young Marquis is married to his beautiful bride, and she is the first to arrive in the garden to strew with flowers the pathway of the bride and bridegroom and all the fine ladies and gentlemen. She runs farther on, and turning, down right, towards the gate, beckons to another girl who now appears by the gate. They whisper together a moment, and then cross to down left, still chattering about the fine dresses of the ladies at the wedding. Two more girls run in, laughing, pause a moment up right. All four run to meet centre, and then throw their rose petals over the path from the gate, for the sounds of the approaching wedding procession are now heard, and the bells are ringing joyously.

Now there enter the first lady and gentleman. Both are very exquisite in the clothes of the most exquisite period in the history of costume, be-wigged, be-powdered, and be-patched. They pass to down centre, she languid, he gallant, and he says :

' Monsieur has married the lady,' and she, her lovely fingers sparkling with jewels as she makes her gestures, replies :

' Ah, she is indeed *charmante*.'

But now the wedding procession itself is here, and the girls run forward to the gate, to strew their flowers before the feet of the lovely little bride, as she comes, so stately in her brocaded dress, with her wig rising above her flower-like face. The young Marquis leads her in so proudly. He is hardly more than a boy himself, eager, young, and slim in his white and silver suit, with his jewelled sword and his buckled shoes. All the conventional dress of the period fails to hide the fact that they are just boy and girl, lovers on the threshold of life. Behind them comes the beautiful figure of the Lady Marquise, his mother, so stately, and yet very human, too, as she looks proudly towards her son. Other ladies and gentlemen fill the stage, making a gay scene such as a Watteau might have painted. And before them all, the Marquis raises his bride's fingers, to his lips, saluting—
' Madame, my wife.' She runs for a moment to his mother, who kisses her forehead, and then back to her husband, who leads her proudly into the house. The ladies and gentlemen

fall back a moment, leaving the way clear to the steps. The Marquis and his bride pass up and out of sight. His mother follows, then the guests, and finally the girls, throwing the red petals over the procession as it passes, and then following into the house themselves. All save the first girl, who lingers, down right, gathering up some of the fallen rose petals into her basket.

B.   But suddenly the whole atmosphere of the scene is changed. For there enters, from up left, a figure, very different from those who have just gone laughing into the house. It is Margot, and she brings with her the shadow of the cloud of menace that is over the land. She enters slowly, as if drawn back irresistibly by fear of what lies behind her, and yet impelled by fear of what lies before.

Again and again she looks back, down the road to the village, and every time returns urgently to the sight of the château, and the pathway strewn with roses, that seem to her sight so like great drops of blood, already shed by the Revolution. She is evidently uncertain what to do and yet urged to something of intense significance. Then she catches sight of the girl down right, and despite her surprise, draws her to the centre.

Very urgently Margot asks : ' Where is Monsieur ? '

And the girl replies : ' Why, he is in the house.'

' Bring him out here,' Margot pleads. But the girl, half laughing, shakes her head. How can she bring him out, when M. le Marquis is celebrating his wedding feast ? She shrugs her shoulders in bewilderment. But Margot continues to urge her more and more desperately into the house, till at last the girl gives up the struggle, and, half pushed by Margot, enters the house to see if she can speak to the Marquis. Margot is left, half mad with anxiety, trying to calm herself to speak to him, to tell him when he comes out, what is threatening them all.

She waits down left.

C.   At last he comes, so slowly and nonchalantly down the steps, wondering who can have called him so urgently from his wedding celebrations, and still with half his thoughts left beside his girl-bride in the house. He does not see Margot at first, but as he reaches the centre she throws herself distractedly at his feet.

' You and Madame must fly,' she urges. He looks at her, bewildered, but still smiling indulgently at the poor girl's obvious distress.

' Why ? ' he asks. ' Why ? '

For answer she takes him by the arm and leads him up stage left, where he can see down the road to the village. He stands looking, and in that moment we see him grow from boy to man. For the thunder-cloud is rolling near indeed. There, along the road approaches a band of the dreaded revolutionaries. Their destination is obviously the château. The Marquis turns and looks towards the house which holds all that is dear to him, a house now given up to merry-making, totally unprotected, save for the toy swords of the few gentlemen among the guests. On one side of him the menace drawing nearer every moment, on the other, his wife and his mother, his own honour, all in desperate danger. Small wonder that he forgets for the moment Margot, who has risked everything to try and warn him before it is too late. She looks at him piteously for protection, but, thinking only of those dear women, whom he must at all costs defend, he passes resolutely into the house. Margot is left alone, and in terror, down left.

D.   Hardly a moment passes before the Leader of the Revolutionaries strides into the garden, a gaunt, haggard, half-starved fanatic, he seems the personification of a people turned to brutes by bitter want and suffering. His very wrongs seem to fill this quiet garden that has known nothing hitherto but gentle thoughts. His great fist shakes the menace of his kind towards the house which holds the hated aristocrats, who make marriages and feast, while the people starve. Gradually the hideous crowd gathers, and their Chief directs them to their positions. Two of them to bind Margot, and to hold her : the wretched girl who thought to warn the aristocrats. Well, she was too late, the Revolution is here. *Vive la Révolution !*

Others he sends into the house to meet those who have entered by the other doors. They are to throw out the cursed aristocrats like rats, until they find that boy they are after, and then——

E. But now the doors burst open, and the terrified guests are flung brutally down the steps to face the revolutionaries. The chief revolutionary stands centre, and as each group of terrified aristocrats tries to rush past him, he threatens or leers triumphantly at them. They are surrounded everywhere, and can only crouch in panic-stricken groups, the ladies like wounded butterflies in their brocaded dresses, the men, swordless and insulted, but shielding the ladies with all that is left to them, their unshakable gallantry. At last two women's figures stand upon the steps. It is the old lady Marquise and her son's wife. Before the dignity of the older woman the revolutionaries stand aside, and the two women pass slowly down the steps together. The Marquis's mother comes down stage right, beautiful and calm, but she sinks upon her knees to pray that the boy may have courage to prove himself a man indeed in this hour of trial. The little bride turns away up right and stands, a drooping figure, struggling for courage in this desperate moment, with her back to the audience.

Last of all appears the Marquis himself. He stands erect a moment at the top of the steps. Then a push sends him down, past the threatening revolutionaries and the terrified women, straight into the leering figure of the leader of the revolutionaries. He stands still before the menacing figure. Twice the man raises his arm to strike the boy, and twice he falls back before the calm disdain in the pale face. But, with a gesture that takes in all the company, he laughs :

' Well, then, *mon brave*, wait for the embrace of Madame la Guillotine.'

A final shudder of apprehension runs through the terrified girls and ladies. The gentlemen turn away in horror at their helplessness ; Margot is crying as she sits, bound, in a far corner. For a moment it seems that the boy's nerve must desert him. So much depends on him, and he is so desperately alone, and all the time so heart-breakingly conscious of the pathetic little figure of his bride, with her happiness fallen and broken on the very day of her wedding.

F.   But gradually the whole atmosphere of the scene changes once more. The boyish figure which is the centre of the picture straightens itself. Monsieur le Marquis stands erect, not a boy, but a man facing life, and death, and making history. A little smile of confidence lightens his face a moment, but is gone again before the stern reality of present action. He turns and faces squarely the half-mad bully standing over him, and the man turns away, sullen and abashed. After all the cursed rat of an aristocrat can't escape, let him do what he likes for the moment. The Marquis walks slowly towards his mother, and stands before her, having first raised her from her knees. There is no need to pray, he has found his courage. She bends and kisses his forehead proudly, and turns away from him. Now he faces the harder task. Behind him he knows his wife is standing. He must face her too with his head high, and leave her alone. He crosses to down left, mustering his strength. Then, very resolutely, he turns and walks to that slight figure which still stands with its back to him. Very gently he lays his hands on her shoulders and turns her towards him. Their eyes meet, and for one moment his courage almost forsakes him. He is on his knees with his face hidden in her hands. But now it is her turn to remember *noblesse oblige*, and tenderly, but not flinching, she raises him to his feet and, as he stands before her, looks straight and courageously at him. He is himself again. They smile at each other, and, not daring to kiss her, lest he fail once more, he looks at her and, with a gesture, says :

    ' Courage and love together are higher than all.'

A bell tolls sombrely far away, and the Marquis turns from his love to the fulfilment of the task in hand. He never looks at his wife or his mother again. Through what follows the ladies and gentlemen and the girls slip silently into the house ; they realize that they are helpless to avert the end which must be played alone by those whom it concerns. The Marquis, his mother and his wife, and Margot are left with the revolutionaries, among the fallen petals which make splashes of red upon the garden path and lawns. The Marquis crosses to Margot. There is no hesitancy about him now, and all the heritage of centuries is in the command of his bearing. He remembers at last that this girl has given her life to try and save his. He will stand by her. He commands the guards to unbind her, which, with a shrug, they do. And all the revolutionaries form two lines from the gate to the centre of the stage.

The Marquis raises Margot to her feet and leads her gently to the centre. He points to the waiting ranks of revolutionaries, and beyond. That is the way they must go. He bends and picks up from the ground a spray of roses which has been lying among the strewn petals. He places it in her hands.

His kindness revives her courage. Margot, holding her roses proudly to her breast, passes down the lines of revolutionaries. For a moment she turns back to smile reassuringly, then she is lost in the increasing crowd.

G. Now, the chief revolutionary steps forward and lays his hand on the Marquis's shoulder, leering, ' Enough of these heroics ; time for you too, my lad.'

The Marquis shakes off his hand, and setting his shoulders very squarely, faces the lines of revolutionaries. Without a look back he walks proudly between them to the gate, and though they threaten, they do not touch him. But as he passes out of sight they crowd, cursing and gesticulating, after him.

The two women are left alone among the fallen, bruised, and trampled rose-leaves. Very slowly the Marquis's mother walks up to the centre back. Her proud head does not bend. But, motionless, she watches and watches and watches the road that leads to death. We know when the crowd has passed out of her sight, for she raises her hand, hardly in a gesture of farewell, but rather as if some part of herself had gone out, seeking a loved one down the long, long road.

The little bride hardly moves from the spot where the Marquis left her. She has seemed like a frozen thing. But now she slips to the ground, with no sound save the dry rustle of the brocade of her wedding-gown. Idly her hands touch the crimson flowers that strew the ground. She gathers up a handful, and as she lets them slip through her fingers, they lie upon her white dress, strangely, like drops of blood shed by the Revolution.

Yet she hardly notices. There she sits, poor little broken white flower, while her eyes, the only things left alive in her white face, go seeking, seeking for her lost love, who bade her be courageous.

NOTES ON MUSIC

Music Required :
   Chopin. Étude. No. 5.
         Preludes. Nos. 4, 6, 14, 17, 18, 20.
         (Published by Augener & Co., Ltd.)

A.   *Étude No. 5.* Play 44 bars, cut 53 bars, play to end
     Entrance of Village Girls, First Lady and Gentleman and Wedding Procession

Entrance of First Girl	8 bars
Entrance of Second Girl. They run to down left	8 bars
Entrance of Third and Fourth Girls. All run to centre and into a diagonal line	12 bars
Entrance of First Lady and Gentleman	8 bars
First Gentleman : ' Monsieur has married Mademoiselle '	4 bars
First Lady : ' She is charming.' Both move to right	4 bars
Entrance of Marquis, Marquise, Lady Marquise and guests	8 bars
Marquis : ' All of you, see, my wife ! I kiss her hand ! ' All bow and curtsy	8 bars
Marquise runs and kisses Lady Marquise and back to centre	10 bars
Marquis and Marquise turn and exit, followed by guests, leaving one village girl	21 bars

B.   *Prelude No. 4.*

         Entrance of Margot

Entrance of Margot. She sees the girl and brings her centre	12 bars

Margot : ' Monsieur, where is he ? '	2 bars
Girl : ' He is in the house '	2 bars
Margot : ' You bring him out here '	2 bars
Girl : ' Oh, no ! '	1 bar
Margot pushes her into the house and goes down left	6 bars

C.   *Prelude No. 6.*

Marquis and Margot

Entrance of Marquis. Margot kneels to him ..	8 bars
Margot : ' You and the lady must fly '	4 bars
Marquis : ' Why ? Why ? '	2 bars
Margot takes him to the gate ; he turns and goes into the house	12 bars

D.   *Prelude No. 14.*

Entrance of Revolutionaries

Entrance of the leader	4 bars
Entrance of two men. They bind Margot ..	4 bars
Others enter and the leader sends two into the house and posts the others on the stage	8 bars
All turn to the house and stand, waiting	3 bars

E.   *Prelude No. 18.*

Bringing out the Prisoners

Ladies or girls cross to centre and then down right	2 bars
Gentlemen cross to centre and up stage	2 bars
Girls or ladies cross to down left	2 bars
Gentlemen cross to centre and then down right ..	2 bars
Lady Marquise and Marquise enter	3 bars
Marquis runs to centre	1 bar
The leader of the revolutionaries threatens the Marquis and reminds him of la Guillotine ..	5 bars
The revolutionaries threaten the aristocrats ..	4 bars

F.   *Prelude No. 17.*

Farewell of the Marquis

The Marquis recovers his courage and faces the leader	18 bars
He crosses to his mother, raises her and crosses down left	16 bars

He crosses to his wife and kneels. She lifts him,
and he holds her hands. He turns with a
gesture .. .. 25 bars
He crosses to Margot. The revolutionaries unbind
her. He brings her to centre .. .. .. 13 bars
The revolutionaries form two diagonal lines, while
the Marquis gives Margot a rose and points to
where she must go .. .. 12 bars
She exits .. .. 6 bars

G. *Prelude No. 20.*

Exit of the Marquis

The leader moves to the Marquis; he turns and
exits slowly, followed by the revolutionaries .. 4 bars
The Lady Marquise moves up stage to watch him go 4 bars
The Marquise sinks down on to the ground.. .. 5 bars

PROPERTY PLOT

Stage :

Rostrum 12 by 4 by 2.
3 tread steps to fit opening of curtains.
2 three-treads at either end of the rostrum off stage.
Plain black or interior backing.
Curtain or garden set.

Hand Props :

4 small baskets filled with rose petals.
1 red rose.

COSTUME

Marquis :

Black buckle shoes with red heels.
White silk stockings.
White satin knee-breeches.
White cutaway coat, in satin or brocade, embroidered with
silver.
Embroidered waistcoat.
Lace jabot with a narrow black ribbon round the throat.
Lace ruffles at the wrist.
Natural-coloured or grey powdered wig dressed straight back,

but not too high, with two rolls at the side, the queue tied with a black *moiré* ribbon.

This type of costume may be worn by all the men, in various colours.

The Bride :

Buckle shoes.

White silk stockings.

Dress in all white, or pale colours.

Embroidered satin petticoat.

The bodice of the dress is cut very low in the neck and trimmed with a fichu knotted in front.

Sleeves to just below the elbow, and finishing in a lace or georgette ruffle.

The skirt open down the front to show the petticoat, and cut with a train at the back.

A natural-coloured wig dressed low on the top and full at the sides, white wig, or unpowdered, short curled hair.

Ladies :

As above in varying colours, or dresses with wide side panniers. Unpowdered hair may be worn dressed closely in curls, with round side wreaths.

Madame la Marquise :

The same style of dress as the Bride, only in a heavy brocade and with long tight sleeves, finished with a ruffle at the wrist. Deeper colouring, introducing purple or green.

Hair : Grey powdered wig dressed fairly high in front, close at the back and with two rolls at the side.

Revolutionaries—Men :

Ragged knee-breeches of dark cloth.

With or without stockings.

Torn buckle shoes or sabots.

Dirty shirts and remains of coats.

Red phrygian caps and tricolour cockades.

Hair : Long and matted.

Revolutionaries—Women :

Ragged skirts of cloth or remnants of finery taken from the aristocrats.

Dirty torn blouses or bodices of any description.

Phrygian caps and tricolour sashes and cockades.

Sabots, shoes, or bare feet with pieces of sacking tied round them.

Margot and the four Peasant Girls :

Striped skirts to the ankle.

Full plain-coloured aprons.

White muslin blouses with full sleeves gathered into a band at the elbow.

Tight-fitting boleros of cloth embroidered all over the front.

Black bonnets with long strings made of silk or velvet worn well back on the head, or lace peasant caps.

Hair : parted in the middle and done in one or two plaits.

Black flat-heeled shoes.

White stockings.

MISS BLOOMER AT BATH

*(To a Collection of Old English Songs. Original Tunes
harmonized by Alex de Jong.)*

MISS BLOOMER AT BATH

The Scene is laid in the Pump Room at Bath, in the 'seventies or 'eighties of the last century, when it was fashionable to be delicate and ' advanced ' to be healthy. One took the ' waters ', and felt that their unpleasant taste ensured relief from those polite maladies which rendered ladies so attractively the ' weaker sex '. But already girls were not what they used to be. They began to play games, in long and well-upholstered dresses certainly, but with surprising vigour. And, in a whisper be it spoken, to ride bicycles in costumes upon which one shuddered to think and dreaded to look.

In this scene we find the old Romance with its sweet old tunes already dying before the advent of the Modern Girl.

The characters are :

> Four Languid Ladies
> Miss Bloomer
> John, a young man
> An Attendant

The scene, as we have said, is in the Pump Room. The entrance is centre back, and up left is the counter, upon which are rows of glasses to be filled by the attendant with the famous waters. The attendant stands behind the counter as the ladies enter.

A.   The first lady enters to down left, the second to up right, the third to down right, and the fourth to up left. They are evidently acutely interested in their languishing selves, and when the last has entered they speak in turn :

First Lady : ' I have such a headache ! '
Second Lady : ' I have the palpitations. Ah ! '
Third Lady : ' I positively swoon with fatigue ! '
Fourth Lady : ' My pulse seems very rapid.'

B.   The attendant comes forward with a tray of glasses. She
goes to each lady in turn, and each takes a glass. One
by one they drink, rather in the manner of elegant birds
at a fountain. Having done so, they wilt once more. ' So
wearing these cures, my dear.'

C.   But now there breaks in upon this picture, so deliciously
feminine, so refined in every way, an apparition that can be
considered as little less than appalling. Miss Bloomer walks
with manly tread, and—no ?—yes ! surely, in a whisper be
it said, divided skirts, into the very centre of the stage.

Quite rudely she refuses the proffered glass of water. With
nerve-racking breeziness she remarks, ' I ride a bicycle.'
But this is not all. Regardless of the distress of the ladies,
she adds without a blush, ' I smoke '; with indelicate freedom
of movement she indicates that she plays tennis ! As she
passes to down left the ladies draw together up right, consoling
themselves as well as may be by remarking to each other,
' Well, at any rate, she will never marry.'

D.   Now their peaceful morning of self-interest is further
shattered by the cheerful entrance of John, a young man of
the town, well known to them all, and undoubtedly delightful,
if ' A little advanced, my dear ; you know what these Oxford
men are.'

He bows with a pleasant air to each lady in turn, and each
hopes that the blush upon her maiden cheek looks well after
the delicate pallor which preceded it. The attendant brings
him a glass of water, and with a wry face, but with the
determination of one who sticks at nothing, he prepares to
drink it. The ladies are suitably interested in what must be
his delicate state of health. ' These athletes are not always
so strong as they look, my dear—and with that fair hair and
bright colour, one never knows.'

E.   When—heavens—that Bloomer girl is going to *speak* to
him. Have they been introduced ? We shall never know.
But certainly she does cross to him, and they shake hands
with a suspicious heartiness. And, worse, she is positively

COSTUMES FOR LADIES
IN 'MISS BLOOMER AT BATH'
(*From 'Punch', 1871*)

inviting him to go for a bicycle ride with her. (Whatever are girls coming to !) And he is accepting. He offers his arm, and, in spite of her emancipation, she takes it, and they go out together, down right. The ladies can only gasp, ' Scandalous ! '

F.   Once the culprits are out of sight, the scandal begins in truth. The ladies walk about, put down their glasses, and talk to themselves, to each other, to any one who will listen. ' Disgraceful ! ' they say. ' A girl displaying her *legs*—on a *bicycle*.' They are almost overcome, their pulse is more rapid than ever. They feel a headache coming on.

G.   When, across the front, where we suppose the Pump Room looks out on to a terrace, pass John and Miss Bloomer, talking confidentially, and wheeling bicycles. The ladies betake themselves as far up to the back as possible, with their backs turned to the scandalous sight. But, as the two culprits disappear, four heads turn round to watch them out of sight, with eyes that are, perhaps, as envious as disapproving. The attendant is frankly admiring.

H.   With one accord the ladies sweep to centre. The attendant is hastily recalled to her duties. Fresh glasses of water are required, and such behaviour should not be stared at by inferiors. But when the girl's back is turned they say in no uncertain gesture, all speaking together, ' She will fall and break her ankle or her head, and that will be the end of *that*, my dear.'

A bicycle bell rings with joyous abandon, and is answered by another.

NOTES ON MUSIC

Note.—The music does not pretend to be of the period of the Scene, but rather to suggest an old-world charm that was passing.

Music Required :

    Old England. English Songs of Long Ago.
       Original tunes harmonized by Alex de Jong.
         (Published by W. de Haan, Utrecht.)

Note.—If there should at any time be any difficulty in

'ADVANCED' YOUNG LADIES
COSTUME FOR MISS BLOOMER IN 'MISS BLOOMER AT BATH'
(*From 'Punch', 1877*)

obtaining this setting of the songs, the little scenes can be enacted to others, as the movements are arranged on the barring of almost any simple air.

A. ' *Advice to Cloe* ' .. .. Mr. Dieupart

Entrance of Ladies (Minuet time)

1st Time :	Play through and repeat	
	First Lady enters	4 bars
	Second Lady enters	4 bars
	Third Lady enters	4 bars
	Fourth Lady enters	4 bars
2nd Time :	First Lady : ' I have a headache ' ..	4 bars
	Second Lady : ' I have palpitations '..	4 bars
	Third Lady : ' I swoon '	4 bars
	Fourth Lady : ' My pulse is very rapid '	4 bars

B. ' *Rosalind's Complaint* ' .. .. Mr. Baker

(To the tune of ' Grimm King of Ghosts '.)

Attendant gives water to 4 ladies	13 bars
They drink	12 bars

C. ' *The Romps Song* ' .. .. Mr. Carey

Entrance of Miss Bloomer

Enter Miss Bloomer to centre	4 bars
' I ride a bicycle '	4 bars
' I smoke '	4 bars
' I play tennis.' Cross down left	4 bars
The ladies : ' She will never marry '	2 bars

D. ' *False Philander* ' .. .. Mr. Jong

Entrance of John

Enter John, to centre	4 bars
Bow to ladies	6 bars
Attendant gives water ; he prepares to drink ..	6 bars

E. ' *The Comparison* ' .. .. .. Set by Mr. Galliard

Miss Bloomer invites John to a Bicycle Ride

Miss Bloomer crosses to John and shakes hands ..	8 bars
She says : ' Will you ride with me ? '	8 bars
He accepts	8 bars
She takes his arm, they exeunt down right. Ladies say : ' Shocking ! '	8 bars

COSTUME FOR JOHN
IN 'MISS BLOOMER AT BATH'
(*From 'Punch', 1876*)

F.   '*The Despairing Shepherd*'   ..   ..   Set by Mr. Gouge

The Ladies despair

Ladies walk about, put down glasses   ..   ..﹣12 bars
They say : ' A girl showing her legs '   ..   ..   4 bars
' On a bicycle ! '   ..   ..   4 bars
They have palpitations, headaches, etc.   ..   ..   3 bars

G.   '*Cupid Mistaken*'   ..   ..   ..   Words by Mr. Prior

Miss Bloomer, John, and the Bicycles

Miss Bloomer and John cross front with bicycles ;
     ladies up to back and look round   ..   ..   16 bars

H.   '*William and Margaret.*'

The Ladies predict the Doom of Miss Bloomer

Ladies to centre   ..   ..   8 bars
' She will fall and break her ankle or head '   ..   4 bars
' And that will be the end of that '   ..   ..   3 bars

Two bicycle bells.

PROPERTY PLOT

Stage :

Interior set, or curtains with entrances centre back, down
right and left. If possible an inner stage, raised, steps
leading down to front stage. Pillars between stages.
(The scene can be played without this.) Counter up left
with glasses (five required in action).

Hand :

Tray	..	..	..	..	*Attendant*
Lady's Bicycle	..	..	..	..	*Miss Bloomer*
Gentleman's Bicycle ..	..	..	..	*John*	

COSTUME

Ladies .

Period 1875–85.
Dresses with not too pronounced ' bustle ' lines.
Skirts elaborately flounced.
Tight-fitting short jackets.

Gloves.

Muffs.

Hair : Dressed in large coil rather high at back, showing the ears.

Small trimmed hats worn well forward.

Black laced or buttoned boots.

Miss Bloomer :

Man's shirt and collar ; tie.

Short fitting jacket.

Divided skirt to the ground.

Ulster to ground.

Plain straw or felt hat.

Black laced or buttoned boots.

Umbrella.

John :

Knickerbocker suit with short jacket.

Low collar, wide tie.

Brown stockings.

Brown laced shoes.

Bowler hat of the period.

Moustache—rather long.

Attendant :

Long black stuff dress.

Apron.

Cap with streamers.

Cuffs and collar (starched).

Black stockings and shoes.

MAD PATSY

(Music by Frederick Bontoft and William Baines.)

This play has been performed at the Savoy Theatre, London, 1922, and at the Memorial Theatre, Stratford-upon-Avon, 1923 and 1924.

In both cases the part of Patsy was played by the author.

MAD PATSY

Patsy, a youth with fine, sensitive hands, knew the song of the birds better than the speech of men. He stole a string of brightly-coloured beads and loved them passing the love of women. So he hid them deep under moss and leaves in a wood, where no man could lay desecrating hands upon them, no woman desire them for herself. He did not know that the People of the Wild are as covetous of shining glass as mortals are, nor did he know that they wear a beauty beyond the human, which tears the heart and burns the brain, and leaves us empty, so that people call us mad.

The characters of this little Scene are :

Patsy, a boy, whom, in the village, they called ' fey '
A Dryad, or perhaps a dream born of a tree

A. The curtain rises on a glade in a wood. We must people it for ourselves with bird and beastie, with tree and flower, shadow and sunlight, while the music hints at unseen shapes, and the quiet of a place of leaves. We just realize that behind the trees forming the background lurks a figure, thin, with pale face and hair, and hunted, animal eyes, when a long white hand steals round a tree-trunk, and the half-glimpsed form is clearly seen a moment. It is Patsy, come from the village to his trees, fearful of the pursuit that ever means mockery for him, irresistibly drawn towards his hidden treasure, the beads—the beads of which he dreams through the unchanging twilight of his days and nights.

Something startles him, and he runs backwards, from the tree against which he stands, looking off right, into the centre of the stage, where he pauses, apprehensive, alert. Are they following him ? He returns to the trees to peer off. But no one is coming and the wood calls—the trees, the sunlight in the leaves, the birds, and the little creatures in the undergrowth. He returns to centre.

Suddenly he points to a mound of leaves below a tree down left. They are there, his darlings, his beautiful treasures, his beads of white and golden glass, that are like sunlight in water and like stars. He runs and kneels beside the mound. Then suddenly he is afraid. They will follow him and see. Then overhead a bird chirps, and he smiles again. 'Yes, yes,' he nods, 'they are here.' Above his head, on the other side, another bird calls, and again he answers with his twisted smile, 'Yes, here; they are here.'

B.   Still kneeling, he flings away the moss and leaves and twigs with which his treasure is covered. He laughs as the dried things soar up into the air and fall away behind him; he is getting near to the ground under which the beads are buried. He pauses, listens. . . . Some one is coming; they will guess his secret. But no one is near, and, using his hands like the paws of a dog, he digs and digs. Then he pauses again, afraid. Something shines against the dark earth, and he draws out a string of glass beads. He lifts them, now this way, now that, in order that the sunlight may catch their gleaming surfaces. He springs to his feet. He circles the stage in a fever of delight. Then he stops centre, and for a moment caresses the beautiful shining things that hold the sunlight. He touches his cheek with them, he holds them to his heart. Now he is whirling with them held at arm's length, making an arc of light about him as he spins. Suddenly he flings them high into the air, laughing to see them strive to reach the tree-tops. Back they fall into his hands. Once more he sends them flying upward, and once more they fall back into his hands and are pressed against his heart.

C.   But now a ripple of thin music shakes the air, and a shimmering form flies past behind him, from among the trees up left, and disappears again up right.

Patsy is wonder-stricken. Who passed by him like a breath? Is his treasure in danger? He limps with his curious twisted walk up left, the place where she disappeared, but there is only shadow and sunlight, and the trees.

Again the thin, floating sound and the flying dryad form.

MAD PATSY

This time she passes from down right to up left, where she remains swaying deliciously, like some young poplar in the golden green of spring.

Patsy sees for the first time the vision of a beauty more unearthly than any glass beads, more to be desired than mortal girls. He follows her to down right and half-way up to centre. She has seen him now, and, moreover, she has seen the beads, the strange shining things of moonlight, sunlight, and water-light. She covets them, longs for them with all the soulless passion of her faery being.

In a moment she is gone again to down left, poised still like thistledown, and he has followed her. Almost he touches her, as her hungry, inhuman hands flutter towards the beads. Then again she flies out of his grasp and is floating, waiting, imploring, up centre.

He follows once more. She begs for the beads. Thinking that if he gives his all she will give herself in return, he thrusts his treasure into her hands. A moment she laughs as she holds their pale beauty in the sunlight. Then she is gone like the sigh of a breeze at evening. She disappears down right.

D. Now all the pent-up frenzy of his darkened life breaks loose. He has lost his vision and his treasure together ; something snaps in him, and for a moment he is all animal in his blind suffering. He rushes madly to the place where she disappeared. There is nothing but a density of leaves. He seeks among the trees down left, up right, in the centre ; everywhere nothingness, and the grave, immovable presences of trees.

He realizes the full bitterness of loss. His hands are empty of the beauty that they held. His heart is empty of the beauty that for a short moment it had loved, his soul is in a dark place, the utter darkness of the animal that is hurt and does not understand.

But with a sudden crying movement he points to the place of hiding where his treasure lay. Perhaps it is still there, undisturbed, waiting for him. Perhaps the treachery of beauty was only one of those dreams that so strangely haunt him sometimes.

He rushes to the spot from which he took the beads originally. Frenziedly he digs again with his hands; but there is nothing, nothing, only earth and leaves—dead leaves.

It is over; the poor bruised heart is broken at last. He rises to rush away from the place of his despair, when, like a lightning flash, realization comes to him. The beads are gone, the vision is fled. But for one moment, he, Mad Patsy, saw the light of beauty and gave to it his all. Nothing was given to him in return, save this knowledge, but that has set him free. His mind is clouded and troubled no longer, as his too sensitive, frail body falls, he goes to meet those others who broke their hearts to find beauty, and smiled to greet it.

A shivering breath floats across the woodland once more, and, as Patsy falls, the dryad flies from shadow into sunlight and is gone again. She does not see him fall; she does not know his heart is broken. She has no heart to break; only in her hands, catching the sunlight like drops of water, gleam the beads that he had loved passing the love of women, but less than the faery form of his own vision.

NOTES ON MUSIC

Music Required :

> *Wood Pictures* .. .. .. Frederick Bontoft
> (Published by Augener & Co., Ltd.)
> *Poem Fragment*, from *Four Poems for Piano*
> William Baines
> (Published by Augener & Co., Ltd.)

A. *Reverie* .. .. Bontoft

Entrance, Patsy Remembers the Beads

Curtain up on empty stage	12 bars
Patsy enters behind trees	6 bars
His hand comes round the tree	4 bars
He enters, backward, running to centre	3 bars
He returns to entrance	4 bars
He returns to centre	5 bars

He thinks of, and points to, beads	4 bars
He runs down to the mound	3 bars
He listens in fear	4 bars
The first bird calls	1 bars
Second bird calls	1 bars
He says : ' Yes, yes '	5 bars

B. *Humoresque* .. .. Bontoft

He digs for the Beads and brings them Out

He flings aside sticks and moss	26 bars
He digs in the ground	23 bars
He stops and listens fearfully	4 bars
' No one is coming '	4 bars
He draws out the beads	7 bars
Holds them in the light on his left	2 bars
Holds them in the light on his right	2 bars
He gets up	2 bars
He runs with the beads	4 bars
Spins round	4 bars
He caresses the beads	14 bars
He throws them up	1 bar
He catches and holds them	3 bars
He throws them	1 bar
He catches them	1 bar

C. *Poem—Fragment* .. .. Baines

The Dryad and the Loss of the Beads

She flies across from up left to up right and disappears	2 bars
He follows to up right	9 bars
She crosses down right to up left	2 bars
He follows her. She crosses to centre. He follows	9 bars
She crosses to down left	2 bars
He follows, nearly touches her. She tries to touch the beads	9 bars
She returns up centre, asking for beads	2 bars
He follows to right of her ; gives her the beads ; holds out his arms to her	10 bars
She disappears down right with beads	2 bars

D. *Appassionata* .. .. Baines

Patsy's Despair

He remains still	2 bars
He runs to down right and cries : ' Nothing ' ..	4 bars

10

He runs to down left and cries : ' Nothing ' ..	4 bars
He runs to up centre, realizes that he is alone and his beads gone	16 bars
Remembers where the beads were hidden	1 bar
Goes down left to mound	2 bars
He digs frenziedly .. .. ' Nothing ! '	4 bars
He digs again .. .. ' Nothing ! '	4 bars
He gets up and returns centre	3 bars
Shows his empty hands and realizes	5 bars
He falls and the dryad flies across the back, left to right	3 bars

PROPERTY PLOT

Stage :

Curtain surround, or cut tree cloth.
Curtains divided into four at back, showing sky cloth.
Mound of leaves, sticks and moss, down left.

Hand :

String of white and yellow, or pale green glass beads.

NOTE.—The beds may be of another colour if preferred, but it should be remembered that red or blue will not show well in blue light, and the scene should not be too brightly lit, suggesting sunlight through leaves.

COSTUME

Patsy :

Short brown knickers.
Light brown or coloured shirt open at neck, sleeves rolled up.
Belt.
Bare legs and feet.

Dryad :

Draperies in shades of green, gold and brown.
Leaves in hair.

THE MOON-MAN'S FAERY RING

A Scene for Children

(Music selected from the works of Grieg and Albert Coates, and ' Nursery Rhymes.')

The play was specially arranged for the children of the Fairy Ring (Children's Branch of the Girls' Realm Guild), and was performed by them at the Scala Theatre, 1927, when the part of the Moon-man was played by the author.

THE MOON-MAN'S FAERY RING

Have you ever seen, when the moon is full, the figure of a slim and shadowy person, with flying hair, just ready to leap from the shining disk of the moon on to a cloud-horse's back? That is the Moon-man. On the night of the full moon he visits the Woods-of-the-World. If you find the Moon-man in the woods on the night of the full moon, he will grant your wish to become the person of your dreams. Everybody wishes, some time or other, that they were somebody else. It's a funny thing, but they do. No matter how comfortable the nursery or their home may be, real children and people always wish they were living another and more exciting life—the life of stories or of dreams.

Well, on the night of the full moon, the Moon-man visits the Woods-of-the-World, and there, if we are lucky enough to see him, our dreams may come true. This play is about some children who did find the Moon-man, and his goblin shoemakers, and their dreams came true for a little while. The goblin shoemakers had to be in the play, because it is they who make the shoes which turn people's feet towards the Paths of Dream.

The scene must, of course, be in a wood.
The people in the play are:

    The Moon-man, who is always young because he is so very old, and yet is always being born again

    The Goblin Shoemakers. They are old too, and have long beards and high pointed red caps. But they are so small that very little children can play them. We all know how little difference there is between a very young baby and a very old gnome

    A Child who dreamed of dancing and Columbine and poetry

    A Child who dreamed of history

Two Little Girls who loved their lessons, but who
    dreamed of the song of birds calling over the
    hills and far away
A Child who dreamed of the days of chivalry
And the People in their dreams
Pierrots, Columbines, and Harlequins
Medieval Knights and Ladyes
An Elizabethan Page

*Scene : Either a woodland set may be used, or a curtain set
with sky cloth, lit moonlight blue, at the back and a cut tree cloth
before it ; or just a set of curtains, which the electrician and our
imagination can easily make believe to be a wood. There is a
moonbeam which follows the Moon-man wherever he goes. The
electrician calls it a ' spot-lime ' which is steel blue, and the
whole scene is flood-blue, with a little pink in it to make that
strange honey-coloured, half-shadowy effect of moonlight.*

A.   As the curtain rises the one ray of moonlight falls upon
a fairy ring in the very middle of the stage. Of course we
think at first that it is made of toadstools, as fairy rings
generally are. But as we look closer, and there's nothing
else to look at for a moment or two, we find that this one is
made of red shoes, set neatly side by side to form a ring.
There are all kinds and makes of shoes, but they are all red.
There are red satin ballet shoes, Elizabethan shoes with
buckles and high red heels, flat Victorian shoes, like our
great-grandmothers wore, made of soft red silk, and the
long-pointed, red, embroidered shoes worn by medieval ladies.
There are other kinds of red shoes too, but those are the
most important, because they come into the story.

But now a goblin march is heard, and there enters from
up left a band of goblin shoemakers, each carrying a red sack
of tools, and led by the Moon-man, a tall, slim, dancing
white figure, shimmering in his moonbeam dress, with his
long white hair blown back by the wind.

He leads the goblins round the stage until they surround
the fairy ring, and then signs to them to sit down to their
shoemaking. The goblins seat themselves in a circle by the

shoes, and, taking a wooden hammer from his sack, each begins tapping busily upon the sole of the shoe which is his job. The Moon-man meanwhile stands behind them, beating time for their hammering.

B.   The music changes, and faintly in the distance are heard the sounds of children's feet and the snapping of twigs. The Moon-man listens. ' Ha-ha,' he thinks, ' there are children abroad this night of the full moon. They've remembered, and are seeking for their dreams. Well, we'll be ready for them. The woods are full of dreams to-night, and all the goblin shoes are ready.' He hastily bids the goblins leave their cobbling. They do so, pack up their tools, and, at the Moon-man's bidding, hide in little, seated, cross-legged groups in the shadows at the back, and at the roots of the trees. They look almost like large red toadstools themselves, but their bright eyes look out from under their red caps expectantly, to see what will come of their shoe-making.

The Moon-man lifts his silver pipe to his lips and, playing a little old-fashioned nursery rhyme upon it, he draws the children out of the shadows. They have evidently escaped from bed, for they are all in pyjamas and nighties, and some still clutch at the favourite toy with which they fell asleep. Woods at night are rather creepy places, and it's nice to have something woolly and comforting to hug. They are five little girls. Two come from up stage right, and three from down stage left. They approach very hesitatingly and are so pleased to meet each other that they run to a little chattering group down centre and peer about anxiously for a moment or two.

The Moon-man has been leading and calling them all the time. But they thought it was the moonlight among the tree-trunks.

C.   Now they suddenly turn and see him standing in the middle of the fairy ring. He points to the shoes. They rush towards them in great delight. They hold them up to show each other, and then put them on. Somehow, it happens that they have chosen the very shoes of the person of their dreams. The child who dreamed of dancing and poetry, has the pair of red ballet shoes. The child who dreamed of history has the buckled shoes worn, surely, by Queen Elizabeth herself. The little girls who loved their lessons have little flat shoes like their great-great-grandmothers, and the child who dreamed of chivalry puts on the embroidered shoes of a medieval ladye. As the children put on the shoes there come, stealing out of the shadows, strange little companies of dream people, who lead the children away out of sight, while the music of their dreams sounds in their ears.

D.　First, from down right, come a little band of Pierrots, Harlequins and Columbines, who, catching her by the hand, lead away the child who dreamed of poetry and dancing into the shadows from whence they came. She follows as if in a dream.

E.　Then from down left appears a page in Elizabethan dress, with a sword upon a velvet cushion. He goes to the child who dreamed of history and, bowing very formally, he shows that she is to follow him. This she does with her dreams of Queen Elizabeth taking shape as she wanders away.

F.　Now there appears, up left, a very prim and proper crocodile of little girls in crinolines and trousers, all reading from little books. The little girls who loved their lessons, but dreamed of bird song, are surrounded by these good little girls and led away up left.

G.　At last a crowd of ladies and gentlemen appear from up right. They seem to have stepped from some old tapestry, for the ladies have long, sweeping brocaded dresses, and steeple hats with floating veils, and the men short brocaded doublets and coloured hose on their shapely legs. They lead away the child who dreamed of chivalry. The children have all disappeared for the moment, seeking their dreams, and the Moon-man has watched them go, smiling to himself to think how moonbeams lighten the human heart.

H.   But now he calls his gnomes together once more, bids them clear away the unclaimed, remaining red shoes, and then sends them back to the tree-roots to watch his games with the dreaming children.

I.   The child who dreamed of poetry and dancing comes back down right. She is dressed now as a real little dancing Columbine, with the frilled skirts of a *ballerina*, and her little scarlet ballet shoes. She is attended by her retinue of Pierrots, Harlequins, and other little Columbines.

Now the Moon-man seems to change. Is he the Moon-man or the soul of all the Pierrots? Surely he is Pierrot. The little Columbine runs up to the centre back, and stands posed as a *ballerina*, dreaming of dancing and all the poetry of Pierrot's love for Columbine. The Moon-man follows her, but she rises on the points of her little red shoes and floats away from him, as if on air. The other Pierrots, Harlequins, etc., have made a little group of players half-way up right. They watch their Columbine playing with the moon, or *is* it Pierrot? He follows her to where she stands poised like a butterfly on a flower, down left ; but she is away again on the points of her little feet, until he catches her down right. Now the Moon-man becomes Pierrot indeed. He says what Pierrot has said to Columbine for hundreds and hundreds of years : ' I love you. Will you marry me ? '

But this little Columbine is off again like the butterfly she once was, and Pierrot is left disconsolate, while she stands up centre back looking half a flower, half a dancer, and very like the dove whose name she carries.

Now one of the small Pierrots comes towards the Moon-man and whispers to him, while he gives him a tight round bouquet of red roses. What he says in that whisper is, ' Give her flowers. She never can resist red roses.' So the Moon-man-Pierrot takes the flowers and, kneeling very humbly beside his flower-like Columbine, offers them to her. She turns to him. Red roses. The flowers of all the dreams in the world. She takes the bouquet, and, looking down upon the kneeling Moon-man-Pierrot, understands the poetry of his love. She pats the top of his bent head, and when he looks up at her again, gives him her hand to kiss. The Moon-man-Pierrot rises to his feet and offers her his arm. Surely those are wedding bells we hear. The other Columbines will be the bridesmaids, the Pierrots and Harlequins the wedding guests, and the Gnomes bring up the rear of the procession as Columbine walks round the stage with her Moon-man-Pierrot. But when they reach the exit down right the Moon-man contrives to slip away and to put the little Pierrot who gave him the roses in his place. Columbine disappears with her dreams of dance and poetry, and the Moon-man is himself once more, laughing with his goblins at the success of his first dream with the fairy shoes.

J. Now, from up left, preceded by the page with the sword, comes the child who dreamed of history. It must of course be she. But at first it seems a Queen Elizabeth in miniature. Her red hair is piled high on her head and surmounted by a very small crown. Her heavy brocaded dress is supported by an enormous farthingale, and a high lace ruffle is round her neck. She walks with great dignity, England's Virgin Queen, Gloriana. But suddenly, in the middle of the stage, she stops. She raises her hands in horror. 'There is a puddle,' she says. 'We cannot proceed.' The page is horror-stricken. But there, by her side, is her ever-gallant Sir Walter Ralegh, looking perhaps a little Moon-mannish, but he swings his moonlight cloak from his shoulder and lays it over the puddle in quite the orthodox manner, kneeling humbly in the mud himself as the Queen passes over. The Queen is pleased. This indeed is one of the gentlemen of England. She signs to the page, who approaches with the sword. Sir Walter Ralegh, or, as we know him, the Moon-man, kneels again before her. She touches him regally upon the shoulder with the sword, and as he rises 'Sir Walter Ralegh' she passes away, bearing the sword of knighthood herself, to other dreaming deeds of queenliness.

The page follows her, and they are gone, down right.

K. As they disappear a band of medieval knights and ladyes appears, up right, with the child who dreamed of chivalry among them. They seem like an old tapestry, or a fourteenth-century Italian fresco-painting. The child who dreamed of chivalry is the chief ladye among them, and as she separates herself from them and passes down stage centre, she finds her own knight before her. It is the Moon-man, but he has found a lance and a pennon on it, and is obviously the perfect knight, about to depart to the Crusades to win glory for his ladye and for the sake of chivalry. She takes a ribbon from her dress and ties it on his arm as he kneels before her to receive his ladye's favour. Then she watches him out of sight as he carries her dreams to far, strange lands of old romance, and she disappears once more among her ladies to the fields of tourneys, feats of valour, and sounds of minstrels.

L.   The little girls who loved their lessons now appear from up left at the head of a most proper crocodile of Victorian little girls. They are now dressed as their own great-grand-mothers, in crinolines and poke bonnets. They have books in their hands from which they are diligently reading. The Crocodile becomes a group, up centre, while the two dreaming children walk very solemnly down centre.

M.   But now the Moon-man has seized his pipe, and plays that enticing little tune of ' Over the Hills and Far Away '. The little girls try to keep their attention fixed on their books, but their heads begin to turn to right and left, looking for the origin of the music. Then the Moon-man flashes by before them. They try to catch him as he passes, but he is gone in a moment, like the ray of moonlight that he is. He dis-appears off stage, down left. The little girls run after him, followed by all the crocodile.

Then he appears up left, and as he dances across the stage he is followed by the children trying to catch him. The gnomes jump up and excitedly follow the chase. They all disappear up right, and when the Moon-man appears a moment later, down right, he has all the other children and their dreams following him as if he were the Pied Piper himself.

He leads them right across the front of the stage and is

once more out of sight, down left ; only to appear again up left with them all at his heels.

N. But this time he leads them into a fairy ring, and the gnomes surround them. One by one their dream-tunes are heard faintly. And, as often happens if you stray into moonlit woods, when you ought to be in bed, the children and their dreams grow suddenly very sleepy. Each little group sinks down to the ground in a sleepy heap, as its tune is heard, until there they all are, asleep in the Fairy Ring, with their heads on each other's shoulders, just tired children, with all the romance, dignity, and chivalry of their dreams forgotten.

O. The Moon-man motions to the goblin shoemakers to sit on the ground around them, and as the curtain falls they take out their hammers once more. While the Moon-man beats time, they begin tap, tap, tapping their fairy spells on other shoes, for other full-moon nights.

How did the children get home ? Well, if you fall asleep in the middle of a dream, haven't you noticed that you always wake up in your own bed, with the sunlight pouring in at the window, and somebody saying it's time to get up ? But, if you're lucky, you remember your dream, and if it was on the night of the full moon you know it was true.

NOTES ON MUSIC

Music Required :

Kobold (Op. 71, No. 3)	Grieg
Old English Dances	Albert Coates

(Published by Elkin & Co., Ltd.)

Nursery Rhymes :

    (a) *Au Claire de la Lune.*
    (b) *Girls and Boys come out to Play.*
    (c) *Lavender's Blue.*
    (d) *Over the Hills and Far Away.*

Detailed barring of each number is not given, as, owing to the possibility of varying the number of children, only a suggestion for the use of the various musical numbers can be made.

A.   *Entrance of Moon-man and Goblins*
    Kobold, first 20 bars   ..   ..   Grieg

        Goblins Hammering Shoes
    Kobold, following 28 bars

        Goblins into Places for Entrance of Children
    Kobold, following 31 bars—no repeats

B.   *Entrance of the Children*
    Girls and Boys come out to Play (twice)

C.   *Children find the Shoes and Put them On*
    Kobold, 20 bars

D.   *Pierrots, etc., fetch the Child who is to be Columbine*
    Au Claire de la Lune (once)

E.   *Page fetches the Child, who is to be Queen Elizabeth*
    Old English Dances, No. 3   ..   ..   ..   Albert Coates
    (' Youths ' only). Cut bars 8 to 16, 23 to 28. No repeat

F.   *Medieval Child is fetched Away*
    Old English Dances, No. 2. Bars 49 to 72   ..   ..   Coates

G.   *' Crocodile ' fetches Victorian Children*
    Lavender's Blue (twice)

H.   *Moon-man arranges the Goblins and calls the Dream Children*
    Kobold, 20 bars

I.   *Scene between Moon-man and Child who dreamed of Columbine*
    Au Claire de la Lune (four times. Last time played with wedding bells for procession)

J.   *Scene with Queen Elizabeth.*
    Old English Dances, No. 3 (twice). Cut bars 8 to 16 and 23 to 28   ..   ..   Coates

K.   *Scene with Medieval Ladye*
    Old English Dances, No. 2. From bar 49 to 72, twice   Coates

L.   *Victorian Children*
     Lavender's Blue (twice)

M.   *Moon-man pipes to the Children. They follow him off, collecting other Children, on, off again, across front, and on into Fairy Ring.*
     Over the Hills and Far Away (ad lib.)

N.   *Children Falling Asleep*
     Medley of all tunes. 8 bars each

O.   *The Goblins sit in Circle round Them. Final Picture*
     Kobold, as required

PROPERTY PLOT

No Stage Props.

Hand :

Off Stage, left.

Lance.	..	..	..	.. *Moon-man*
Sword	..	..	..	.. *Elizabethan Page*
Cushion	..	..	..	.. *Ditto*

Off Stage, right.

Bouquet	..	..	..	.. *Pierrot*
6 hammers	..	..	..	.. *Gnomes*
6 red sacks	..	..	..	.. *Ditto*
6 pairs of red shoes		..	..	.. *Ditto*

Coloured ribbon for Medieval Ladye.

Off Stage at various exit dresses for Columbine, Queen Elizabeth, Medieval Ladye and 2 Victorian children.

COSTUME

The Moon-man :

White tights.
Silver, or blue and silver tunic with long tight sleeves.
Blue silk wig, dusted with silver powder, or white wig, with rather long hair, blown backward.
Blue and silver cloak.

Columbine :

    Pink tights and red ballet shoes.
    Short pink ballet skirt with tight-fitting bodice.
    Small wreath of pink flowers.

Pierrot :

    White pierrot suit, shoes and stockings.
    White ruff.
    Black skull-cap.

Medieval Ladye :

    Long dress with train, high waisted with jewelled waistband.
    Neck of dress cut to a low V back and front and trimmed with
        fur.
    Long, tight-fitting sleeves.
    Steeple head-dress with veil.

Queen Elizabeth :

    Brocaded dress with a wheel farthingale.
    Embroidered and jewelled stomacher.
    Puffed and jewelled sleeves.
    High ruff-collar.
    Pearl cap and wired veil.
    Red ' Elizabeth ' wig.

School Girls :

    ' Kate Greenaway ' dresses.
    Mittens.
    Pantalettes.
    White stockings.
    Black sandals.

Gnomes :

    Brown tights and jerseys.
    Red gnome shoes.
    Red pointed caps.

Medieval Men :

    Tights.
    Brocade tunic, short and full.
    Jewelled belt.

Puffed and slashed sleeves.
Tunic laced across chest showing white shirt.
Velvet 'flower-pot' hat.

Elizabethan Page :

Orange tights.
Brown velvet flat-heeled shoes with orange rosettes.
Brown velvet trunks slashed with orange.
Brown velvet doublet slashed with orange.
Ruff.
Flat hat made of brown velvet with orange feather.

BED-TIME RHYMES

(A Series of Nursery Rhymes arranged as simple action scenes for Children. To the Music of 'A Children's Overture' by Roger Quilter.)

BED-TIME RHYMES

This series of Nursery Rhymes is arranged to interpret the 'Children's Overture' by Roger Quilter as a succession of related scenes. But each rhyme can be taught separately, and, if required, so produced with a singing accompaniment taken from any version of the Nursery Rhymes in the order given, or with the music as suggested in the notes.

Any number of children can take part. We divide them into Boys, Girls and Babies. There is one Grown-up, whom we will call the Dame, because she must play that part in 'Dame, get up and bake your Pies'. The rhymes can be performed on a stage, when no setting is required but a simple background of curtains, or in a class-room.

A. The curtain rises during the introduction on an empty stage. The first tune to be interpreted is, 'Girls and Boys come out to Play'. The words we have to mime are :

> Girls and boys come out to play,
> The moon doth shine as bright as day ;
> Leave your supper and leave your sleep,
> Come to your playfellows in the street.
>
> Come with a whoop, and come with a call ;
> Come with a good will or not at all ;
> Up the ladder and down the wall ;
> A penny loaf will serve us all.

The first child, either boy or girl, enters up left, joyously skipping. He calls at each entrance up right, down right, down left, and, as he passes each, some of the other children join him, dancing happily after him, until they are gathered in a group, centre. Then they speak in gesture : ' Come with whoop and come with call,' and describe in gesture : ' Up the ladder and down the wall.' Next they sit on the ground, all except the first child, who holds up the loaf of bread he has been carrying. He hands out pieces among the children, who jump up once more and dance in a circle, finishing with all the girls up centre back, the boys in a group down centre. All throw away the remainder of the bread they have pretended to eat while dancing.

And we are ready for the next rhyme which is :

B.
Upon Paul's Steeple stands a Tree

Upon Paul's steeple stands a tree,
As full of apples as can be.
The little boys of London Town
They run with hooks to pull them down ;
And then they run from hedge to hedge
Until they come to London Bridge.

The boys pointing say, ' Up there is a tree ', and make a gesture describing the apples. ' We go and pick them ', and they run right and mime pulling down the apples, with which they proudly go to up centre back ; while the girls come forward in two lines, and, with hands joined, make a bridge. The boys pass over ' London Bridge ', their hands full of imaginary big red apples. They divide right and left, where they go off. The girls remain centre, where they sit on the ground.

Now the Dame appears up left, ready to begin :

C.
Dame, get up and bake your Pies

Dame, get up and bake your pies,
Bake your pies, bake your pies ;
Dame, get up and bake your pies,
On Christmas Day in the morning.

Dame, what makes your ducks to die,
Ducks to die, ducks to die ;
Dame, what makes your ducks to die,
On Christmas Day in the morning ?

Their wings are cut, they cannot fly,
Cannot fly, cannot fly ;
Their wings are cut, they cannot fly,
On Christmas Day in the morning.

The Dame sweeps towards the group of little girls, centre, saying, ' Get up, get up,' and by a gesture of stirring something in a basin says, ' Make your pies.' The girls jump up and mime stirring, rolling pastry, and other indications of cooking, finishing by passing up to the back with their pies prepared for the oven. We now turn to the question of ducks. One boy enters as himself, the others limp on, down left and right, as very lame ducks. The boy goes to the Dame and, indicating the ducks, asks what ' makes them to die ' ? The girls run down to comfort the poor ducks, and they say, ' Their wings are cut, they cannot fly,' and remain stroking the poor maimed creatures (who are much consoled for such unheroic parts by large yellow beaks which they put on before entering for this rhyme).

But quickly the ducks recover, the beaks are cast aside, and we prepare for :

D.

I saw Three Ships come sailing By

I saw three ships come sailing by,
Sailing by, sailing by ;
I saw three ships come sailing by,
On Christmas Day in the morning.

Three pretty girls were in them then,
In them then, in them then ;
Three pretty girls were in them then,
On Christmas Day in the morning.

And one could whistle and one could sing,
The other play on the violin ;
Such joy there was at my wedding,
On Christmas Day in the morning.

The Dame says, ' I saw three ships go sailing by.' Just to be sure that we know what the rhyme is about, she produces a paper boat and tells us that three like that went sailing by. While she is doing this the children make three boats, one child kneeling at each end and two at the sides, with joined hands. In each boat stands one of the bigger girls. (If there are not enough children to make three boats we can manage quite well with one, but it must have three girls standing in it.) The boats rise and fall on the rhythm of the music, as if sailing on the sea.

The Dame continues, ' In them were three pretty girls.'

(And we see them standing there.) 'One did whistle,' and there she stands, whistling joyfully. 'The second did sing,' and the second girl raises her hands to make her voice carry in the wind, and mimes a lovely song. 'The third did play the violin,' and there she is, playing away as the boat rises and falls on the waves.

All look very joyous indeed as the Dame signifies that it is her wedding morning.

The boats break up and the children all stand in one or two lines, facing the audience for :

E.   *Sing a Song of Sixpence*

Sing a song of sixpence, a pocket full of rye.
Four and twenty blackbirds baked in a pie.
When the pie was opened, the birds began to sing.
Wasn't that a dainty dish to set before the King ?

The King was in his counting-house, counting out his money ;
The Queen was in the parlour, eating bread and honey ;
The maid was in the garden, hanging out the clothes,
When down came a blackbird and pecked off her nose.

The children, all together, mime, 'Sing a song' and 'Sixpence' ; they tap their pockets to show they are 'full of rye'. They show us 'twenty-four birds' in 'a round pie'. They show the cutting of the pie to open it, and the 'birds began to sing'. They lift up the dish and set it before the King. All this is mimed in descriptive gesture on the rhythm of the music.

Now we need four 'principals'—two boys and two girls. They stand in a line thus :

The Queen.   The Maid.   The King.   The Blackbird.

The King shows us how he is counting out his money in his counting-house.

The Queen eats bread and honey with great dignity in the parlour.

The Maid hangs out the clothes in the garden, when—the Blackbird hops out from behind the King's counting-house and pecks off her nose (his two hands forming a hungry beak for the purpose). The Maid is left lamenting, the Blackbird swallowing with suspicious gusto, the King and Queen horror-stricken at the catastrophe. Those children who do not take part in this verse form a ' chorus ' watching each character in turn, and are duly horrified by the loss of the maid's nose. We finish with a procession carrying blackbird pies triumphantly until all disappear leaving a clear stage for :

F.

There was a Lady loved a Swine

There was a Lady loved a Swine.
  ' Honey,' said she ;
' Pig-hog, wilt thou be mine ? '
  'Hunc,' said he.

' I will build thee a silver stye,
  Honey,' said she.
' And in it thou shalt lie.'
  ' Hunc,' said he.

The Dame, now being a beautiful lady, enters, amorously, from up left. One of the boys as the ' pig-hog ' from down right. They meet centre. She declares her love, and says, ' Will you marry me ? ' He replies rudely, ' Hunc,' and no more ; but he listens, piggishly, as she continues, ' I will build you a *lovely* stye ; will you go into it ? ' But again he merely replies, ' Hunc,' goes slowly off down right, registering disgust with all lovely ladies. She exits disconsolately up left.

Now a sound of piping is heard, and we know it must be :

G.

Over the Hills and Far Away

Tom he was a piper's son,
He learnt to play when he was young ;
But all the tunes that he could play
Was ' Over the hills and far away '.
Over the hills a great way off,
The wind shall blow my top-knot off.

Tom with his pipe made such a noise,
That he pleased both the girls and boys ;
And they stopped to hear him play
' Over the hills and far away '.
Over the hills a great way off,
The wind shall blow my top-knot off.

One of the boys, as Tom, enters playing his pipe to himself. He stands centre, thinking of the wind on ' the hills a great way off '.

Then right and left and up and down he pipes to call the boys and girls. He leads them round the stage ; he leads them away out of sight and back again ; off the stage and on again ; until, finally, they all disappear as the piping dies away in the distance.

Then there enter

H.
The Frog and the Crow

A jolly fat frog lived in the river Swim, O !
A comely black crow lived on the river brim, O !
　' Come on shore, Come on shore ! '
Said the crow to the frog, and then, O !
　' No, you'll bite me ! No, you'll bite me ! '
Said the frog to the crow again, O !

The frog began a-swimming, a-swimming to land, O !
And the crow began jumping to give him his hand, O !
　' Sir, you're welcome ! Sir, you're welcome ! '
Said the crow to the frog, and then, O !
　' Sir, I thank you ! Sir, I thank you ! '
Said the frog to the crow again, O !

' But where is the sweet music on yonder green hill, O ?
And where are all the dancers, the dancers in yellow ?
　All in yellow. All in yellow ? '
Said the frog to the crow, and then, O !
　' Sir, they're here ! Sir, they're here ! '
Said the crow to the frog . . .[1]

The crow stands stiffly upon the bank, half up right. The frog ' swims in the River Swim, O ! ' down left. The crow, making gallant gesture with his wing, says : ' Come on shore ! Come on shore ! ' And the frog, after a doubtful moment, says, ' Yes, I will. Yes, I will.' He swims towards the crow, who greedily holds out a wing to help him on shore. The frog lands with a jump beside the crow. They bow ceremoniously to each other. The frog is about to ask his question about the music and the dancers, when—' snap '—the crow has swallowed him, with a jump. ' Very good,' says the crow, and exits backwards. So we never see that the frog is really hidden behind him, and was not swallowed at all !

And now another froggy story :

[1] Here the crow swallows the frog.

I.   *The Frog he Would a-wooing Go*

A frog he would a-wooing go,
   (' Heigh-ho ! ' says Rowley.)
Whether his mother would let him or no,
    With a rowley, powley, gammon and spinach,
    ' Heigh-ho,' says Anthony Rowley.

' Pray, Mistress Mouse, are you within ? '
   (' Heigh-ho ! ' says Rowley.)
' Oh, yes, kind sir, I'm sitting to spin.'
    With a rowley, powley, gammon and spinach,
    ' Heigh-ho ! ' says Anthony Rowley.

Now the end of this rhyme is rather sad, so we have changed it to another version, in which Mr. Rat, after first refusing his consent, joins the hands of Mistress Mouse and Froggy, and they all depart to a delicious wedding-breakfast. So the action is like this :

The Frog enters eagerly from up left, and Mistress Mouse, knitting a trifle feverishly (she was a busy little thing, you remember, from the spinning mentioned in the rhyme, but spinning is difficult to mime). Froggy says, ' I shall marry the lady,' and advances towards her. He bows, she curtsies demurely. He says, ' I love you.' Her little grey whiskers twitter nervously, when Mr. Rat enters angrily centre, and says, ' What's all this ? ' Then Froggy says, ' I love her,' and Mistress Mouse squeaks, ' I love him.' So Rat relents and joins their hands. Moreover, he adds, ' We will have a great feast.' He gives an arm to Mistress Mouse, and an arm to Froggy, and they all exeunt, very cheerfully, down left. Which, I think you will agree, is a much better ending than the one where everybody is eaten cruelly by some one.

And it goes beautifully to the music.

J.   *Baa ! Baa ! Black Sheep*

' Baa ! Baa ! Black Sheep, have you any wool ? '
' Yes, sir ! Yes, sir ! Three bags full ;
One for my master, and one for my dame,
And one for the little boy that lives down the lane.'

There enter from up left and right the Dame, and a boy impersonating the black sheep. They meet centre, and the Dame questions the sheep. He nods his head, saying, ' Yes,

yes,' and shows in his mouth three bags of wool. Standing on three legs, he gestures with the fourth, saying ' One for the man, one for the lady, and one for the little boy over there.' Sure enough here comes the master for his bag, the lady for hers, and the little boy for his. They take their bags from the sheep's mouth and carry them away.

The Dame and the sheep exeunt together, she patting him for a good, industrious, wool-producing fellow.

Now it is time for the babies to do something by themselves, so we have :

K.   *Here We go Round the Mulberry Bush*
                  Here we go round the mulberry bush,
                  The mulberry bush, the mulberry bush.
                  Here we go round the mulberry bush
                  On a cold and frosty morning.

                  This is the way we clap our hands,
                  Clap our hands, clap our hands.
                  This is the way we clap our hands
                  On a cold and frosty morning.

The babies enter, skipping, and form a circle centre. They clap their hands in time to the music. Then they skip round the mulberry bush, and finish sitting in a circle. This isn't a very big mime, but you see the babies are very little, and if we learn to skip and clap our hands in time to the music, that is as much as we can expect when we are only three or four years old. Besides, it's nearly bed-time and we want to play :

L.   *Oranges and Lemons.*
          ' Oranges and Lemons,' says the bells of St. Clement's.
          ' You owe me five farthings,' says the bells of St. Martin's.
          ' When will you pay me ? ' says the bells of Old Bailey.
          ' When I grow rich,' says the bells of Shoreditch.
          ' When will that be ? ' says the bells of Stepney.
          ' I do not know,' says the great bell of Bow.
          ' Here comes a candle to light you to bed,
          And here comes a chopper to chop off your head.'

All the boys and girls come on from right and left. The two biggest make an archway up centre. The other children come through the archway, playing the game in the usual way, each of the first ones takes a baby by the hand from the group centre, and they all continue passing under the arch, singing as they play, if they like. Then the Dame enters with a lighted candle, and tells them they must all go to bed like good children.

But the tune of ' Girls and Boys come out to Play ' is heard again, and the children break away, skipping, running, and playing, in all directions. But at last the Dame collects them once more, and there they stand drawn up behind her in a very proper crocodile, the tallest in front, down to the last and smallest baby ; the very littlest of all she holds by the hand. When the crocodile is ready, she leads it off round the stage. Then she stands centre ; the children break away for a moment. But the curtain falls on the picture of them all clustering round the Dame for a good night hug, or perhaps it is for the very last story. Just *one* more—please.

NOTES ON MUSIC

Music Required :

    A Children's Overture .. .. .. Roger Quilter
            (Published by Winthrop Rogers, Ltd.)

Introduction. Curtain on last 2 bars.

A.   *Girls and Boys come out to Play*
      Entrance of first child followed by others. To group
          centre .. .. 8 bars
      ' Come with a whoop and call ' .. .. .. 4 bars
      ' Up ladder and down wall.' All ready for loaf .. 4 bars
      Giving out bread .. .. 8 bars
      All up .. .. 5 bars
      Dance in circle—girls up to up centre ; boys throw
          away bread and down centre .. .. .. 10 bars

B.   *Upon Paul's Steeple stands a Tree* (Boys)
      ' Up there is a tree with apples. We pick them ' .. 8 bars
      Up to back, girls make bridge ; boys walk over it
          and exeunt .. .. 8 bars

C.   *Dame get up and bake your Pies*
      Introduction : Dame, to centre, speaks to girls.
          All up .. .. 6 bars
      Stir and roll and up to back.. .. .. .. 8 bars

Boy to Dame—other as ducks—' What's the matter
with them ? ' .. .. 8 bars
Girls to ducks : .. .. 4 bars
' Their wings are cut ! They cannot fly.' Stroke
ducks .. .. 8 bars

D.   *I saw Three Ships*
Dame : ' I saw ships three go sailing by ' ; others
form boats .. .. 10 bars
' There are three pretty girls ' .. .. .. 4 bars
(1) Whistles, (2) violin, (3) sings .. .. .. 6 bars
' I marry.' All up into line .. .. .. 4 bars

E.   *Sing a Song of Sixpence*
   1st Time.
' Sing a Song of Sixpence, pockets full of rye .. 4 bars
' Twenty-four birds in pie ' .. .. .. 4 bars
Cut pie. Birds sing .. .. 4 bars
Lift pies and up to back .. .. 4 bars
Principals to places .. .. 4 bars
Repeat 20 bars.
   2nd Time.
King .. .. 4 bars
Queen .. .. 4 bars
Maid .. .. 4 bars
Blackbird .. .. 4 bars
All into procession, round and off .. .. 6 bars

F.   *There was a Lady loved a Swine*
Entrance, up right and up left.
She : ' Will you marry me ? '
He : ' Hunk ! ' .. .. 8 bars
' If I for you build a sty, will you go in ? '
' No ! ' Exit .. .. 10 bars

G.   *Over the Hills and Far Away*
Tom enters to centre and play .. .. .. 12 bars
Call children and lead on and off, etc. ; finish with
exit .. .. 48 bars
Preparation for next rhyme .. .. 2 bars

H.   *The Frog and the Crow*
Enter to down left and up right .. .. .. 4 bars
Frog swims .. .. 4 bars
Crow—straight wings .. .. 4 bars
' Come here ' .. .. 4 bars

'Well, yes!' .. .. 4 bars
Frog swims. Crow jumps. Holds out wing .. 8 bars
Frog on shore. Both bow .. .. 8 bars
Crow swallows frog. Exit .. .. 16 bars

I. *Frog he would a-wooing Go*
Enter frog, up left .. .. 7 bars
Enter mouse, up right .. .. 4 bars
Frog, 'I marry her.' Go to her .. .. .. 5 bars
He bows. She curtsies .. .. 5 bars
He : 'I love you.' She is coy .. .. .. 4 bars
Enter rat : 'What's this ? ' .. .. 8 bars
Frog : 'I love her.' Mouse : 'I love him ' .. 6 bars
Rat joins their hands.. .. .. 8 bars
Rat : 'We have a banquet ' .. .. .. 4 bars
Gives arm to each and exit .. .. 8 bars

J. *Baa ! Baa ! Black Sheep !*
Enter up left and right. ' Have you any wool ? '
'Yes !' Three bags in mouth .. .. 8 bars
One for man ; one for lady ; one for boy over there 8 bars
Enter man and take bag .. .. 4 bars
Enter lady and take bag .. .. 4 bars
Enter boy and take bag .. .. 4 bars
Exit all.. .. .. 8 bars

K. *Here we go Round the Mulberry Bush*
Run and skip in circle .. .. 10 bars
Clap hands .. .. 4 bars
Round again and sit .. .. 10 bars

L. *Oranges and Lemons*
Entrance. Make arch ; play .. .. .. 18 bars
Enter Dame : ' You go bed ' .. .. .. 14 bars
Children away .. .. 14 bars
Call into crocodile and ready .. .. .. 12 bars
Walk round and picture .. .. 16 bars

PROPERTY PLOT

Stage :
Simple curtain set.
No furniture.

Hand Props :

Loaf of bread, with inside taken out and loose pieces put back	*First Child in ' Girls and Boys '*
False beaks (or masks)	*Ducks in ' Dame get Up '*
Paper boat	*Dame in ' I saw three ships '*
Penny whistle or shepherd pipe	*Tom in ' Over the Hills and Far Away '*
Crow's mask Frog's mask } (optional)	*' The Frog and the Crow '*
Frog's mask Mouse's mask } (optional) Rat's mask	*' The Frog he would a-wooing Go '*
Black sheep's mask, (optional) 3 small bags of wool	*Sheep in ' Baa ! baa ! Black Sheep ! '*
Practical candle in candlestick	*Dame in ' Oranges and Lemons '*

COSTUME

Each producer will have his or her own ideas as to the most effective way to dress children, so no actual list of costumes will be given here. Some will favour a Kate Greenaway style, some the children's own dresses—cotton frocks for the girls in bright colours ; knickers and shirts for the boys. But there need be no question of dressing each of the characters in the rhymes as the parts they represent, except with masks, as suggested in the property list. Only if isolated rhymes are performed would this be practicable. The Dame should wear a costume in which she will look suitable in her various parts, that is, not too ' modern ', while not necessarily setting the whole in a particular period. On the other hand, a charming ensemble could be made by choosing some old-world period and dressing the Dame, girls, and boys strictly within it. This must be for the producer to decide.

PRINTED BY
JARROLD AND SONS LTD.
NORWICH